EVOLUTION OF AN ANGLER

DUNCAN CHARMAN

First published in November 2012

Editors: Rosie Barham and Terry Doe

ISBN number: 978-0-9572559-3-7

Unit Four, Ashton Gate, Harold Hill, Romford, RM3 8UF

Designed and published by m!press (Media) LTD.

This book is dedicated to my parents.

Acknowledgements and special thanks

From a very early age my parents spotted my love for nature, butterflies, birds and flowers, but more importantly fish. I needed no encouragement to venture outdoors and Dad's enthusiasm for angling became infectious. Mum was happy to have some space, allowing her to bake cakes, and when we returned after a successful day never moaned at washing fish-slimed clothes, as well as having a hot meal on the table.

I might not have been the 'Master of Arts' at school, but common sense I did have, and it was this that allowed the art of watercraft to be understood and slowly learned. It's not just when I was young that they looked after me; they're still doing it now, and it's from the deepest place in my heart that I thank them for encouraging me never to give up on a passion and for following a dream. Making a living out of angling might not be the most highly paid, but for me fresh air is worth far more than crispy notes, and they know that.

I see myself in my dad, and if I still have the enthusiasm and desire to venture out when I've passed 80, and look as good as he does, well I will die a happy man.
Thank you…

Friends and family
A massive thank you to Chris Charlton, Andy Mutchmore and Mervyn Hudd for putting up with my competitive nature. The company and banter we've experienced throughout our angling careers will never be forgotten.
Steve (Donut) Ansell for his never-ending enthusiasm, capturing memorable moments on film and helping with proof reading chapters as well as his contribution to the content of this book.

Steve (Blobby) Larkcom. Without your in-depth knowledge into 'what's in where', many of the specimens I have landed along the way would never have happened.

My brother, Kevin, who from a very early age has been my angling companion and best friend...long may it continue.

And finally to my girlfriend who understands my passion and love for the sport as well as putting up with the countless hours that I'm away.

Photography

Chris Ponsford – Image 8 in Chapter 31.

Pat MacInnes – Opening shot of Chapter 21 and F1 brace shot in Chapter 30.

Roy Westwood – Net of dace and chub, Chapter 30.

Steve Partner – Bream brace shot, Chapter 20.

Mel Smethurst – Grass carp in Chapter 31.

Sponsors

Korum and Sonubaits (Preston Innovations)

Although many would say I had earned my worth, I still feel extremely fortunate to have been associated with one of the best fishing organisations in the country, Preston Innovations. Having worn the logo on my sleeve for over five years, it was such a shame that my worth wasn't recognised in the later years as it had been in the beginning.

Wychwood

My first sponsors. At the time, it was respected anglers such as Colin Davidson, Simon Scott and Paul Garner who initially saw my potential and passion, then approached me with the view to being sponsored. It was a big step and an honour to be accepted and I thank you all for spotting me.

Contents

The early days

I was just five when my father first took me fishing. It was to a small pond run by a local club, no more than an acre in size, called Hartley Mauditt, a few miles from my home in Alton, Hampshire. This little lake was where Dad taught me the rudiments of angling and the art of watercraft, especially the importance of following the wind, along with honing my float-fishing skills.

Dad as a young man landing a bream on the River Huntspill.

Back then, the pond was rich in *Typha latifolia* better known as common bulrush, *Iris pseudacorus* and a small-leafed, yellow-flowering water lily, and every now and again I would watch, fascinated, as a big bronze head surfaced and slurped in some unexpected insects from within the plants. These monsters were wild carp; long, lean, fighting machines, yet catching one was a long way off. However, I knew my day would come.

The pond was full of beautiful rudd and this was the first fish that I caught, and it's probably why they are my favourite species to this day. A few big perch were also present along with tench and bream that had

been imported from Holland. Sadly, shortly after stocking, they all died, but before doing so, they spawned, allowing for the species to add some diversity to our catches.

From that first outing, Dad had to take me and my older brother, Kevin, with him every time, and although the pond was tiny it created a never-ending adventure for the two of us. Gradually, over the years, our knowledge of the pond grew and with the strength of our tackle increasing, I knew that one of the massive wild carp would finally grace my net, and I vividly remember the day it did.

I was watching a small peacock waggler when it disappeared and on lifting my short fibreglass rod I found it almost ripped from my hands. The surface erupted as an angry carp ploughed through numerous lily pads. Eventually, the unseen monster surfaced and slid into my tiny landing net, and although only around three pounds, it seemed humungous to me.

When Dad wasn't going to Hartley, we would grab our rods and walk to the Caker Bridge Stream on the outskirts of Alton. It's one of the tributaries that create the source of the river Wey and it would dry up in the summer months, leaving all the fish to congregate in a small pool under a bridge. We spent numerous hours under this bridge where we would use tiny pole floats and maggots to catch minnows, sticklebacks and bullheads and if we were lucky, a stone loach.

Sadly, the wild carp at Hartley were lost, unable to compete with the mirrors and commons that were stocked. The bulrush and iris also died being replaced with the large-flowered common lily and as a result the numbers of rudd, tench, perch and skimmers drastically diminished. The carp had taken over and as a result had populated the lake to the extent that they had become stunted. A netting to remove them revealed another species, one that had up to this time remained unknown; crucian carp, and after this thinning out

they became a frequent visitor to the bank. I even remember winning a match with over 20lb of them from the big lily pad in front of the church. Roach were also introduced, which only added to the difficult environment for the beautiful rudd.

As we grew older, Dad would give us a lift to the water, leaving us alone for a few hours before collecting us later in the day. It was a time when the pond held a monster mirror and it was this fish that Kevin and I would angle for, using big pieces of floating crust. This carp was always found within the bulrushes situated in front of the church and was eventually caught by Kevin at a weight of 7lb 12oz. I'm not sure how many times we went on to catch this fish, but I remember that the tactic after hooking it was to let it dive into the bulrushes. Once it stopped, we would wade into the lake, through the rushes, sending up masses of smelly bubbles released from the silt, until we found her.

Dad taking an afternoon nap.

We learned to pose with big fish at an early age.

My learning ground, Hartley Mauditt.

Having a great knowledge of the pond, we progressed into match fishing. It was a learning curve, yet the competition and the thought of winning a few quid from the pools captivated our minds and as all good match anglers do, soon found an edge that saw us winning a high percentage of the matches held on the water.

The edge was trout pellets. Until then, everyone used maggots, bread or sweetcorn on running line but our newfound wonder bait had the small carp crawling up our rods, and when poles were introduced, we were one of the first to be using them. I can remember the look on the faces of the older anglers when Dad dropped us off as they knew they would struggle to frame. In fact, the match attendance seemed to drop during our reign. I even remember hearing a noise behind me while fishing below the high bank and, turning round, spotting one of the competitors crawling on all fours to try to spot what I was using; unfortunately for him this was covered with a towel.

At the age of around seven, Dad managed to get rights to fish an old estate lake called Awbridge Danes, not too far from Romsey. It was owned by Wilf and Joan Stainer and along with another angler, Frank Banfield, Dad would occasionally allow us to join them. It's as if it were yesterday. I can still visualise the gates to the shingle driveway that led to a small parking spot which was surrounded by a rickety, rusty metal fence. The house was within a stone-walled courtyard and peacocks wandered around, along with a golden pheasant that lived in a cage. My memories of that lake are of colourful rhododendrons surrounding it, and dense woodland behind, along with an old stone boathouse surrounded by lilies.

Most of OAC yearly trophies.

Apart from the distinctive, loud call of the peacocks, Awbridge was extremely peaceful, the smell of the woodland was intense, and while we sat on the boathouse we would watch massive golden orfe drift between the vegetation. I wasn't lucky enough to catch one of these huge orfe but Kevin did, one weighing around 4lb, and looking back, in 1970 this would have probably broken the British record!

Dad and Frank were more interested in the lake's population of tench and I recall Dad cutting a new swim out of the rhododendrons one summer, then baiting it for days, only to take the lake apart and catch what we later found out to be almost the lake's entire population of tench.

My most memorable catch was a giant eel taken on lobworms and it was this fish that probably embedded my love for the species, something that I would find out about later in my angling career. Sadly after three, maybe four seasons, the lake suffered from an oxygen deficiency due to an algae bloom, and its population of tench, roach, pike and orfe were lost.

We had arrived to fish on that fateful morning and I remember seeing the bottom of the lake around the overflow was littered with dead roach. The eels could be seen everywhere, in between the branches of the overhanging rhododendrons where they managed to get their heads out of the water; some were even making their way across land to a small stream at the bottom of the woodland.

Our family summer holidays were usually spent in a tent and it was on these vacations that Dad introduced us to sea fishing. I can't remember catching much, but do recall catching eels, wrasse, and a bass off Pembroke Harbour; trying to catch shoal bass in the tidal river at Barnstable and sitting on the shingle at Slapton Sands watching the tip of Dad's carp rod, hoping that a flounder or two would grab his ragworm.

Another holiday, this time in the luxury of a caravan was spent on the south coast close to Hastings. Fishing a narrow tidal canal, Kevin and I would catch small eels and take them back to the caravan where we ate them after grilling them with butter in foil.

Finally, it was time to move on and the next angling club we joined was Oakhanger. This seemed a massive club compared to Hartley Mauditt and even had its own junior section. Wednesday evenings, after school, we would run around organising our tackle and bait before Dad would take us to either Kingsley or Shortheath Pond where we would compete in the Junior Matchman series. In those days it was all about float fishing and it was floats such as the Stillwater Blue that did the damage.

Onions and Carbonite floats were also used and small cubes of meat seemed to catch the better fish. Dad had taught us well, as our consistency saw us winning the odd match as well as the trophy on numerous occasions. However, we did have some competition and I remember the names of two other anglers who gave us a run for our money, they were Richard French, Steven Peters and Patrick Birkby.

I stayed a member of Hartley for many years and remember, as a teenager, being allowed by my parents to fish the night along with my angling friend, Mickey. Hartley Mauditt is mentioned in The Domesday Book, and the pond rests next to St Leonard's Church, which is all that remains of a hamlet that once stood there. I believe that the manor house was destroyed in the days of the plague. The pond is rumoured to be haunted by the ghost of a headless horseman who would come out of the pond on misty nights, so this was always on our minds.

Sheltering under an umbrella that had a canvas overwrap draped across it, we watched as the mist increased and darkness fell. Sometime in the night, a big splash was heard along with massive ripples extending across the lake. This was followed by another and at first we thought that someone was dismantling Mickey's Fizzy motorbike and throwing it in. Slowly, the splashes came closer and I recall being so frightened that I froze, holding a penknife in one hand. Mickey was in a similar position yet plucked up courage after a twig was trodden on behind, to jump up to see what was behind the tent, which turned out to be my brother clutching a breeze block. Kevin and his friend had stolen a few from a building site and knowing it was a misty night and that we were fishing the lake, created a plan to scare us senseless; something they succeeded in doing.

Progressing from the junior section at Oakhanger, we found ourselves up against the adults and again on Wednesday evenings would fish the senior matchman series held either at Kingsley, Shortheath or Rookery.

By this time, Kevin and I knew the waters well and for a few years we dominated these matches. I remember one AGM held at Alton's Community Centre when it became a bit embarrassing for the club official as the two of us cleaned up every trophy, apart from the RNLI Trophy, which seemed to elude us.

Floating baits were finally banned, but not before we'd exploited them, and during one match I remember Simon Gould chanting comments across Rookery after taking five carp to my two on the tactic. He was somewhat quieter when I weighed in 28lb to his 26lb, though.

My role in match fishing heightened as I took on the position of match secretary as well as organising teams to compete in the Central Southern League, held on venues such as the Arun, Rother and Wey. These matches were often tough, fished throughout the winter, sometimes when the river was up and scratching around for anything was usually the case. Certain species were banned, which infuriated me, as I always felt that if a fish was caught fairly then it should be counted, yet on the Rother, grayling, trout, pike, eels and even minnows didn't count and I recall one match on this river at Woolbeading where I caught seven species, yet only weighed in 10oz!

Kevin at Frensham with over fifty tench.

Once again, the urge to progress saw the family joining Farnham Angling Society. It was around this time, at an age of around 20, that my match fishing days ended as it was a period when carp puddles started to become popular. I do recall fishing an open on the River Loddon at Sindlesham, where anglers would turn up for the draw, and then if they didn't pick the bream pegs, numbers 49 or 86 would leave and head off to another draw; the river was that predictable.

What I loved about fishing the rivers was trying to find where the fish lived in the swim allocated, and then skilfully trotting a stick down a crease to catch. Unfortunately, the rivers were on the decline and catch results were poor, attendances began to fall and I was forced to venture on to the newer commercial carp fisheries. Having no ban of the quantity of bait that could be used, it soon became apparent that whoever fed the most, caught the most. It seemed that the skill of angling had been lost and I slowly drifted away from the match scene.

I was working as an engineer in Kingsworthy during this period and it was here that I would spend my lunchtimes feeding the trout in the crystal clear water of the river Itchen. Unfortunately for the trout, it wasn't long before these became destined for the table as armed with a handline I found myself removing them and selling to the inspectors. The traditional close season, where both lakes and rivers were closed for a three-month period was also being exploited, and when FAS decided to stock Badshot Lea Big Pond and allow any-method trout fishing, my extra income continued. Let's just say I arrived with a five-tube rod holdall, yet I only had one rod!

We had made a few friends while at Oakhanger AC, namely Simon, Lenny, Dickie and Cottie. They had also moved on and joined Farnham AS and knowing we weren't interested in their target - carp - encouraged me and Kevin to try Frensham Great Pond. Venturing on to such a huge water after being used to small club lakes was extremely daunting, yet on my first-ever outing and after being handed a few small strawberry boilies from Simon, I caught my first tench.

At the time I thought it was a big crucian. Now I have other ideas.

Hair rigging was new to me, so all I did was side-hook one and using a waggler cast out to a batch of bubbles that I hoped was from a tench. I was fishing a swim called the Corridor, two down from the gate below the main car park and can see to this day the red top of the waggler disappearing.

Those early days were spent targeting the lake's huge population of tench. Standing out in the lake wearing just shorts and trainers we would float fish all night, watching an isotope on top of a loaded waggler, spraying corn around this and cursing near two-pound roach. This may seem odd nowadays but back in the late 80s a 6lb tench was considered big, far superior to us than a near 2lb roach and we had to wade through dozens of these before connecting with our quarry.

Rudd were also present, and the best I caught was 1lb 10oz, but roach dominated and every night, as we stood in the lake, the shoal could be spotted moving toward us from the left, eventually settling over our baited spots. It was always the bridle path opposite the hotel we fished, usually the last six swims before the conservation area below the main car park, yet this area only seemed to produce at night, whereas the bank in front of the A287 seemed to fish during the day.

Even the rain never dampened our spirits at Frensham.

Slowly, we started to move around and the conservation area to the left of the small beach became a favoured spot. Tactics here were to place a platform well out into the lake then fill our blue Shakespeare match boxes with water, along with a few bricks, then fish the swingtip and bread over a big bed of groundbait. The tench fishing here was incredible and most days when a westerly blew into this bank, 100lb was a realistic target.

Around this time, three other anglers became close angling companions, Chris (Jiz) Charlton and Andy (Munchie) Muchmore as well as Merv the Perv. Just to embarrass me and my brother, they called us 'The Topper Twins'; I will leave this to your imagination.

Probably the biggest catch of tench we ever made was on a hot summer day. Kevin and I had set up on the only platform in the lake, situated near to one corner, among a stand of high reeds. As soon as we arrived and looked out, it was clear that the majority of Frensham's tench were in front of us, although at first we thought they were sunning themselves and unlikely to feed. Kevin fished the tip and bread while I cast a waggler using corn. I think we lost count after 58, and when you think, back in those days they averaged 5lb, the total weight was incredible.

The platform was also the swim that produced my biggest-ever Frensham tench, one that weighed 8lb 2oz. There were a few other strange captures; one was a crucian carp weighing 3lb 10oz that remained my personal best for many years, as well as a rainbow trout and in more recent times, a bream, caught by Adrian Eves. A few carp were also taken, mostly while feeder fishing with bread, but these were fish in the low-teen bracket and the much sought-after fully-scaled never made a mistake by taking one of our tench baits.

The pike fishing was also good, but even back in those days a 20 was classified as a big fish for the venue, and ever since Rick Gardner took a 30lb specimen from the water, it has always been in a steady decline.

The perch had also disappeared by the time we arrived, due to the disease that almost wiped them out across the country in the mid-80s, but Dad often related stories of how prolific these were, and especially off the beach where he would use a small spinner with a lobworm trailing from the hooks. Fortunately, perch have made a welcome comeback and thrive in the water today and one of over 2lb doesn't raise any eyebrows. The beach area also had added benefits during the hot summer nights and on more than one occasion I watched as young girls stripped off and went skinny-dipping.

We had moved on from using swing-tips and by now were using more specialist equipment, including bite alarms along with using small, tutti-frutti boilies next to method feeders over the brilliant Expo groundbait. Even in those days, we were being watched, often approached, and when an article appeared in the press starting with the words, 'I walked the lake the night before and found tench rolling in an area', we were somewhat taken back, as it should have started, 'I set up in a swim fished and baited by the regulars the previous night'!

Kevin with Mr Blobby from Carters.

Numerous further memorable sessions were spent on Frensham, including the night Merv and I had a bad attack of wind, only to be confronted by an angler requesting that we grew up, which turned out to be a fellow workmate from the engineering company we both worked for. Then there was the evening when Kevin pushed a barbed baiting needle an inch into his fingertip, only for me to refuse to take him to hospital as I was catching too many tench. Luckily, Munchie was also fishing and given the task. The fishing was always fantastic, as was the company, and to this day,

whenever I hear the track by the Communards, 'Don't leave me this way', my mind drifts back. I remember that it was this track being played late into the night by the hotel's DJ.

Ireland was to become a regular angling holiday; first with Kevin and Dad, then later with Munchie, Merv the Perv, and Simon. Staying at McAllister's in the town of Ballinamore, we fished venues such as Lake Garadice, as well as rivers such as the Shannon, Bann and Suck and the Grand Union Canal near Athy.

The competitive nature of my angling never left me and we decided to hold a yearly species challenge that would see the losing team buying the curry and beers. Nine of the main species were on our target list and the biggest of each led to an overall weight total. Kevin teamed up with Chris, and Andy with me; they were called 'Team Invincible', while we were 'Team Toss', well, that's what they called us.

I'm not too sure how many years this competition lasted, but I do know that it didn't cost me much, well, not in curry or beer, as we would usually win. The last year though we did lose, as on the very last day of the season they needed a barbel, while we felt a 20lb pike would clinch victory. That day, I caught a pike weighing 19lb 15oz from Carters, while Chris took a 7lb barbel from the backwater at Sindlesham.

The other venue that gave me some diversity was the River Loddon, around Carters Hill and Sindlesham Mill. Throughout my match fishing days and beyond, the only species that really interested me regarding size was pike, and when Munchie called to say that he had just witnessed a huge Esox attack his feeder while fishing Peg 49 at Sindlesham, my brother Kevin and I had to investigate.

Pike were always on my mind. A twenty from Carters.

It was the start of a period of tremendous pike action that, apart from Thorpe Park, has never been equalled, as numerous big pike fell over the next few seasons. Peg 49 was always the banker, along with peg 10, as well as a deep drop-off just below the bridge, an area we called the rocks.

The biggest pike I landed from the stretch weighed 25lb 14oz, but there were rumours that a 30 had been caught. A scraper 20, that we called 'Mr Blobby', was a regular visitor to the bank, named because it had a big red boil on its tail, but my most memorable catch was a brace of 20s taken in the company of my best friend, Glen, who sadly passed away after a long battle with breast cancer when he was just into his 30s. He was always my good-luck charm and although not a fisherman, he had a passion for keeping koi carp and loved coming out for a few hours. It was with him that I initially hooked and landed a 23lb 13oz pike from the rocks, before moving to peg 49 and taking one of 25lb 4oz. Sadly, as with many pike waters, our captures leaked out, and after yet another feature in a weekly magazine that made the venue look easy, it became popular, and as we all know pike don't take kindly to pressure.

Scours Lane on the Thames. Big bream country.

One of seven caught on caster under a stick float.

Barbel were also featuring in our catches. The most remarkable was one weighing 8lb 7oz that took a liking to a sardine fished on snap tackle from peg 10 in February. Even stranger was that the following year, in the same swim, using the same bait and method, and in the same month, I took another weighing 9lb 1oz, probably the same fish!

We did catch barbel on more traditional tactics, although not what's classified as traditional today, but I remember a session while fishing the pole in Peg 51. Using a worm and maggot cocktail, a couple of tench and bream had graced my net before the elastic started leaving the end of the pole at an alarming rate. These fish were lost, yet one that decided to stay deep and slow was finally landed, and weighed 7lb 6oz.

Another stretch of the Loddon that we visited regularly was at Shinfield. It was run by Cove Angling Club and although we weren't members, we used to get exchange tickets from Farnham AS. The going swims had been located during a club match against Cove. Unbeknown to me at the time, I had drawn the flyer, but after five hours I had little to show for my efforts. The far bank offered a crease, one that I had neglected due to a fallen tree to my left, on the near side.

The Cove angler to my left started to catch quality roach late in the day and a chance cast to the far bank saw me attached to one as well. Unfortunately, it was one of those occasions when I read the swim incorrectly, yet a few quality roach towards the end of the match, as well as seeing the angler downstream win, revealed a hotspot of which we would take full advantage.

Being young and able to wake early saw us arriving well early. Parking my apple green Opel Kadett on the bridge, we would initially drop the tackle off in the swims, well before dawn, and then retreat to the car. When the first car woke us, we would simply walk to the swims and start fishing.

The roach fishing was spectacular. Holding back on the pole, we would initially see small roach appear, yet after balling it in, they would steadily grow. The best we took from the stretch weighed a shade over 2lb, taken by Kevin, yet roach approaching this were commonplace and nets exceeding 40lb weren't unusual.

Another contributing factor for the decline of the pike on the Loddon, and probably the roach, and an increase in barbel, was the lowering of the water level. Before this, the river wasn't that weedy and had beds of lilies down each bank, but with the Environment Agency wanting to encourage salmon to migrate up the river this was done, yet to this day I haven't heard

The barbel that loved a sardine!

of a salmon being caught. Tench were also caught regularly as were carp, which could be tempted using dog biscuits between the lilies.

Although we fished numerous other waters, such as Wellington Country Park where we would catch 100lb of tench on red maggots throughout the winter, and the river Wey through Farnham, the only other venue that stands out is the Thames. Initially, we fished the Promenade at Caversham where we caught good bags of roach, dace and perch, yet it was the big bream around the island downstream of Scours Lane at Tilehurst that I loved fishing.

Other venues on the Farnham portfolio were visited; Mill Lane, Potbridge, River Valley, Stillwater, Badshot Lea Big Pond and Tarn to name a few, along with stretches of the Loddon run by Farnborough Angling, and stillwaters such as the Hollybush Pits.

Sadly though, as we get older, time seems to become limited. Kevin married as did Chris, both having kids and not really wanted any of this, my father became my closest angling partner. Would I change it? Not in a million years. Our adventures on the Thames and beyond will live with me forever.

The roach fishing on the Loddon was incredible.

A friendship to this day

FAS Tarn Pond (Cut Mill)

It was late June, the country was bathed in glorious sunshine and, for me, there was only one place to be - Farnham Angling Society's Tarn Pond. I knew that the carp would be well up for a floater or two.

Typical Leney taken on an exploding bag.

Standing thigh deep within the lake I scanned the water in front of the Moat swim for signs of carp. There was absolutely no wind and the water was dead calm, yet every now and again the odd carp would surface, lips first, slowly sucking in the odd floater that I'd catapulted out just moments before. Slowly, their confidence grew and the clever Leneys that had seen everything in the past, dropped their guard and competed for every morsel that was floating above. Periodically, I would catapult out a mixture of pellets, some very small, and it was these that whipped the surface into a feeding frenzy on numerous occasions.

It was time to cast in, so I propelled a small bubble float, half-filled with water, well beyond the feeding fish and eased it back slowly, so not to disturb them. I knew my chance was moments away and as I watched the doggy biscuits like a hawk, I saw a pair of lips surface, inches away, and then they were gone. I didn't wait for the float to move, but struck and watched as the surface erupted. With rod bent double and clutch screaming, I smiled as static anglers around me watched, for I was in my element at that precise moment. A few minutes later, a heavily-scaled mirror weighing about 15lb was admired before she was slipped back into her watery home.

The feeding routine commenced and after 40 minutes it was time to make a cast, once again, but the moment was interrupted as a series of bow waves put me off my stride. They were coming from the direction of the next swim, Double Reeds, and my first thought was that the much sought-after carp known as 'Scar', usually around the 30lb mark, had just launched itself clear of the water, but I was wrong. To my right, another floater angler was making his way out into the lake and he turned out to be Steve 'Donut' Ansell, a passionate Tarn angler who had also heard that the Leneys were having it off the top.

This is where it all started; a friendship that has grown stronger with time, and although we may not fish together as much as we did back then, our passion for angling is as strong as ever, and when we do catch up it's a pleasure that we both cherish. I can't recall if I caught another fish, but I do remember watching Donut, who I later found out was a chef, carefully catapult floaters out as if he was preparing a meal fit for the Queen. It wasn't long before he was bent into a fish of a similar size to mine, and after a quick photo we sat chatting and a friendship was born.

I only lived a couple of miles away and sometimes I'd steal an hour or two in the middle of the day when conditions looked favourable. On numerous occasions, I would either find Donut already positioned out in the lake, or arriving soon after. It was as if we both knew when conditions were right. I'm not sure why others weren't doing the same but it seemed that the two of us were the only anglers taking the opportunity to catch off the top. It was something that only seemed to happen once every six years or so, and by the time others cottoned on that the carp were feeding off the top, it was either too late, or they thought they could catch in this way the following year, only to find that the carp ignored everything on the surface.

My most rewarding session was while standing in the Cottage swim. I had two hours to spare and in this time had taken seven fish off the top, including a scraper-20. What made it more enjoyable was that by wading well out into the lake I was able to use my trusted 13' Normark Titan Match rod; not exactly what it was designed to do, but perfect for quickly picking the line off the surface on a take and setting the hook.

Looking back, my records show that I set mirror and common carp personal bests that year, both weighing 23lb 11oz as well as a best leather of 17lb 1oz, all taken off the top, and strangely, Donut had also taken his best floater-caught common weighing 23lb 11oz.

Over the next few seasons, our friendship grew and although the carp rarely showed an interest in floaters during this time, we both caught plenty of them using contrasting methods. I became known as Gobber as I would use small, exploding bags of Active 8 crumb next to a 14mm boilie that I would initially place in my mouth before dipping it into GLM powder, Green Lip Mussel, no GLM (personal joke that will make Donut chuckle). It was a tactic that worked time after time and on occasions I would turn up, cast at a showing fish, catch and then leave, all in the space of around 30 minutes. No wonder I wasn't very popular with a few of the regulars!

26lb 4oz catfish taken on one of Tarn's memorable sessions.

While I fished for one carp at a time, Steve would do the opposite. In fact, I thought he wanted to attract every carp in the lake, as kilo after kilo of bait would be introduced. I became known as Mr Consistent as most nights one or two carp would fall. Steve would normally get a good night's sleep, yet on the odd occasion, all hell would be let loose in his swim and he would be catching constantly, having what's known as a red-letter day.

One session that I will always remember was on the 2nd of August, 1999. Steve and I had been targeting catfish at Badshot Lea Big Pond, on conventional cat baits; however, we had become disillusioned with this approach as, time after time, a carper would catch what we were after, a 20lb cat, on boilies. I needed a change of scenery, so ignoring the job in hand, we decided to head back to Tarn for a spot of boilie fishing for carp.

Here are the actual words taken from my diary of the session...
Tarn, Monday August 2nd – 3rd 1999 – Peg 6, The Birch.

Red-letter day. Started at 6.30pm. 7.30pm, first run resulting in a 10lb 10oz mirror. 9.30pm, second fish which was Popeye at 25lb 2oz, a new personal best. 10pm, landed a catfish of 26lb 4oz another personal best. At 6.15am landed Pole at 26lb 5oz, upping my best once more, and then at 8am took my fifth fish, a mirror of 13lb 15oz. All fish came to Active 8 with GLM mouth-dipped coated boilies. South-easterly, humid night and very dark following hottest weekend of the year. Kevin fished The Bog also taking five fish on Active 8, carp of 11lb 7oz, 13lb 8oz, 13lb 7oz, Small Lobe at 21lb 8oz and Black Spot which also gave him his personal best weighing 22lb 10oz. Donut was next door and managed one mid-double, and was kept busy for his photography skills and supplying the cigars after each personal best. What a night!

Scar was the most sought-after carp; an age-old Leney that although not the prettiest, was one of the biggest and by far the most respected. Donut managed to catch this fish twice, both times at big weights and I remember vacating the High Bank swim one evening, knowing that I had fish showing all over my baits, only for him to call me the following day with tales of Scar at over 30lb. To be honest, I don't recall being obsessed with weights back then, catching was far more important, yet I did feel it was my time to take one of the big girls, especially after catching far more than most did over the years. However, my name, Mr Consistent, soon changed to The Pest Controller, especially after the summer of 2000 that was spent on Stillwater, another venue run by Farnham Angling Society.

I'm not going to spend too much time on this campaign, as I was well and truly beaten up, but Donut seemed to catch wherever he placed a bait. It was a period of his angling career that was kind to him, a time when he was in his element, in tune with the venue and he proceeded to take the place apart. All the known fish fell to his tactics, that were identical to mine as I had soon copied his after a few captures, yet something he was doing was different and fish such as the Pug and Penny graced his net. I hooked my fair share, but seemed to be blessed with hookpulls and I recall one morning when I played a deep, heavy fish all the way to the net, only for the inevitable to happen. Days later, Donut hooked and landed Penny at over 30lb and in her mouth was a fresh hook hold; mine probably!

Donut's catches on Stillwater included the lake's most sought-after carp, Penny.

On another occasion, once again, I played a fish until it was right under my feet, only for it to find a snag. Looking back, I think this was one of the rogue catfish that had somehow found their way into the lake.

The last session I want to mention was one while I was fishing The Pads. Donut arrived late and doubled up, but I was smiling as I had my baits positioned in the best spots and knew his were unlikely to be touched. A 24lb mirror on the wrong side of the lens proved me wrong!

Although, at the time I was seriously questioning my ability to catch, I look back and smile as this campaign taught me loads. Something Donut was doing created an edge, and I think it was his persistence in casting close to the lilies from the canal bank that made the difference. I felt that I was casting as close to them as he was, but I have since watched Donut cast, and he has a much flatter cast than me, so his baits shot further under the lilies than mine.

It was also a period when friends were made and one such angler, and a friend to this day, is Mick Barnes. He was also witnessing Donut rip the place apart, but he was the middle man here because he had far more carp than I did.

Donut's catches on Stillwater made up for my consistent catches on Tarn and although he was well up for another season on the lake, I wasn't, and decided to head back to Tarn the following summer. Knowing that Donut is a social angler, I knew he would agree and, once again, much to the annoyance of the odd regular, we returned.

The carp were once again up for surface baits and we enjoyed a summer of catching bliss. Then, come the cooler months when they dropped back down, we had the tactics and knowledge to continue catching. At the time, we were oblivious to how some anglers looked upon us; although not the most prolific catchers on the venue, we were still a threat to some, and unbeknown, the green-eyed monster was hovering.

We had a really good time that summer and I remember a chap walking down to the lake one evening and on reading the sign, 'night priority swim', stripped off and went for a swim! I was rolling around laughing as Big Dean and his mates shouted unrepeatable words at him, only for him to completely ignore them. When the odd 3oz lead started landing around him, though, he soon made a quick escape!

Scraper-20 taken off the top.

Another night saw Big Dean opposite my position in Double Reeds, yet unbeknown to the bailiff we had a very good understanding. The club ran a rule that no angler should cast further than 50 per cent across the lake, and that was fine with me, but on casting my rig, probably 45 per cent of the distance, I was harangued with abuse from the opposite bank. Moments later, the bailiff appeared and gave me a ticking off, one that I took, although I asked him how he could gauge the 50 per cent rule. As he left, Donut positioned his new toy, a fart machine, in close proximity and enjoyed letting rip with a few loud farts as he departed, or should that read, 'de-farted'?

Don't get me wrong; although we had a good laugh, fishing was without a doubt the most important reason for us to be on the lake. Donut's knowledge of the lake's inhabitants was bordering on insanity. They were like pets, and if either of us had ever seen or felt that the lake or what it held was in danger, then we would have been the first to step in and protect it. Unfortunately though, catching fish on a regular basis comes at a cost and we were soon to find out the hard way.

More carp were caught, including probably my most notable catch from the venue during the many enjoyable years spent on the water. It was during the

At last! Scar, but not looking her best.

Typical Leney taken on an exploding bag.

really cold winter of 2001. I'd set up in my favourite swim, the Birch, and opted for using corn as a hookbait. In the early hours, my alarm sounded and I recall falling out of my sleeping bag in utter disbelief as Tarn was one of the hardest winter waters I knew and getting a bite was almost unheard of. Amazingly, one of the venue's big ghostie commons had made a mistake and weighing 25lb 1oz, it had a few heads turning. It wasn't the last memorable capture of that year, though, as on the 4th of August, Scar finally picked up my bait. She weighed 27lb 7oz and was far from her best and well down in weight, yet as I said, size really didn't matter back then.

Donut's fart machine was put to good use between takes, and many a dog walker became embarrassed as it went off when they walked by, only for us to look at them in complete disgust. In fact, one bailiff even found himself having to think about taking his dog to the vet as we convinced him that his pet was unwell. It was also a time when Donut was getting wound up due to a common carp, well in excess of 30lb, that was attracting anglers. All they were interested in was this fish, with no respect for, or knowledge of, the lake's other residents, proper old Leney strain carp. It was then that I realised just how passionate this guy was.

Given the chance to fish for an original mid-double Leney, or a brought-on fish that's 40-plus, well, it was a no-brainer for either of us. It was just a crying shame that the club didn't realise this at the time and tried to get him more involved with Tarn's history.

The laughs finally came to an end though, as in August that year the club changed the telephone number needed to book on to its night ticket. For countless years, we had abided by the system without question, but because I'd moved house, the newsletter informing me of the change never arrived. Amazingly, the club had left the old telephone booking number going to voicemail, something that I still don't understand to this day. It was this that caused the confusion. If that number had been disconnected, then we would have instantly realised that there was a problem and made the necessary calls to find out why. However, after numerous calls, only to be confronted with voicemail each time, I left a message saying that Donut and I would be fishing Tarn on the 13th of August.

Without going into too much detail, the bailiff on that night was quite happy for us to stay, but the head bailiff wasn't. The rules state that anyone fishing after 10.30pm needs a code, obtainable from the night ticket operator, something we obviously knew about, tried to get, and yet didn't have. Waiting for the head bailiff to arrive so we could discuss the problem, we were amazed when he drove into the car park at 10.10pm and parked up. Even back then, I knew that a bailiff needed to be diplomatic, so when he waited until 10.40pm to confront us, you can imagine the situation. Having been advised of our predicament and knowing that the bailiff on the

night was happy for us to stay, he still insisted we leave. It was a truly sad moment in both our angling careers and for a month or so we worried about which way things would go. However, with the feeling we were going to be banned, we decided that we wanted to be remembered and the chance presented itself later that month. We were making the most of what could be our last days on Tarn when from the opposite bank we heard the same undiplomatic bailiff laughing about our situation and what he wanted to happen to us at the disciplinary meeting the following night. Well, as you can imagine, we were getting a bit hot under the collar on the opposite side. It was then that Donut entered my swim, not in a very happy state, but as I was calming him down, we created a game plan that would see the bailiff on the receiving end of a practical joke.

Mysteriously, catfish had found their way into the lake and if any were accidentally caught we were requested to place them within holding tubes, and club officials notified before they were removed. With the young bailiff on the far bank, Donut and I played out the ultimate catfish capture, knowing that this would be heard across the lake. Screaming alarms, followed by clutches slipping, landing net handles splashing the water, and flash photography, had everyone fooled into believing that a true monster had been landed.

I remember Kevin walking into the swim, shaking his head.
"Guys, is this going to help your cause?" he said, and then, "Do you realise the bailiff's calling you from across the lake?"
Er... "Yep!"

Well, with the invisible 30lb catfish landed, we watched as a head torch started to make its way hastily around the lake, followed by another, heading in the opposite direction and we laughed, imagining the bailiff's predicament.

A few moments later, we were confronted not just by the bailiff but also the fishery manager. They were desperately looking into my landing net and asking, 'where's the cat?' By this time, I had reeled one rod in and rested it against the oval, wetted myself down, as well as the unhooking mat, and lit a bloody great cigar that Donut had passed to me. Well, as you can imagine, it didn't do us any favours but we were still giggling the following night when we found ourselves in front of the executive committee.

That night we were told that both of us would be facing a ban for not obtaining a night code, and although it was upsetting at the time, little did I know that it was to be a pivotal point in my angling career; as they say, 'when one door closes, another opens'.

To this day, I haven't fished the lake for carp. I just don't feel comfortable on the venue, which is such a shame, as it is a beautiful place and one full of memories.

An eel goldmine
Mill Lane

The following chapter, written by Steve Ansell, was titled 'Eel today...Gone tomorrow' and was originally published in Pike and Predators, in August 2002.

When Steve Ansell chanced upon a local water that showed promising early signs of big eels, he and his angling friends began to feel that they'd discovered a gold mine. In a relatively short space of time there followed a remarkable series of memorable eel captures for all concerned.

'I suppose my love for *Anguilla anguilla* first blossomed in about 1993 when I caught one of 2lb on a small roach deadbait at Rotherfield Pond in Midhurst, after seeing a young lad catching them to sell to the local Chinese takeaway. I then dabbled around locally, managing to catch a few up to 2lb 4oz. Then, during a carping trip to a pit near Aldershot in the summer of '99, I bumped into a guy called Simon, who was the Southern Regional Organiser for the Anguilla Club. He told me that he'd caught eels to 3lb 8oz, and he was sure the lake held some bigger ones. My passion was awoken again. The carp soon took second place and my fascination for the 'water snakes' was rekindled.

Along with my fishing partner, Duncan 'Topper' Charman, and his brother Kevin, we had a little bash at the eels in the Aldershot lake. It was here that I had first used lobworms as opposed to just small deadbaits. We also used dendrobaenas, but had hardly any runs using them, and they also attracted numbers of small bream.

We did catch our fair share of eels, but missed far more runs than we connected with; on one particular night I missed twelve runs. This was to be an all too familiar occurrence during the rest of my eeling days.

My biggest from the venue was a new PB of 2lb 9oz. Topper's best was 3lb 10oz, Kevin's 3lb 14oz and a friend of ours, Munchie, caught a 3lb 6oz albino (quite rare, I imagine).

As summer turned to autumn and the first frosts of the year arrived, the takes began to dry up and we came to the conclusion that Kevin's eel was probably the biggest in there, although we had heard of a mid-four, but there were no pictures. News came of another lake that was rumoured to contain some biggies, but it had not produced one for years, not even to the carp boys using fishmeal boilies, as is the case on most eel-infested carp venues.

On May 9th 2000, Topper and Kevin did an overnighter at the lake in question. Kevin had, just day's prior, stalked one of the venue's much sought-after carp, The Dink, weighing over 33lb and taken on 8lb line and breadflake, so was on a high and full of confidence. It was 27° during the day, overcast and muggy; a perfect night for eels, thinking back. I was already there, trying my hand at stalking some of the lake's big carp. I managed a grassy of about 14lb and was just packing up when the brothers arrived.
"We're going to have a bash at the tench and bream tonight. Meat and lobs should sort them out," said Kevin.
"You never know, we may have a chance of one of the rumoured big wrigglers," joked Topper, knowing full well that there hadn't been one out for years. I had a girl on the go at the time and with other things on my mind that evening wished them an eventful night's angling and left them to it.

At about 8am I was awoken by the Monty Python theme emitting from my Nokia. I answered the phone, still half asleep.

"Bingo!" shouted Topper down the phone in such an excited manner that I sat bolt upright, knocking my good lady's coffee all down her front. After administering first aid, I was able to listen to what the ecstatic Topper had to say.

"They exist!" he exclaimed. "Kevin started off with a 7lb pike on the meat at 6pm, and then at midnight it all went off. Missed runs left, right and centre, real screamers too!

At first we thought they were tench, but they all came to the worms. Then in the early hours, Kevin connected with one, it was an eel..."

"Well, how bloody big was it then?!" I blurted. "Five pound six! **** me!" I yelled, now getting so excited that my lady friend had gone downstairs to avoid any further injury.

"Doesn't stop there, mate. Minutes after that I landed one of five-four, and lost one of similar size at first light. I'll see you at the tackle shop at midday, let's get equipped for a proper campaign. Who knows what we'll have!"

Kevin with the much sought after Dink from Mill Lane.

The first eel from a new venue is always special.

With that, he said his goodbyes. He didn't even wait for my reply, because he knew he'd see me at the shop. We'd both caught the bug again and all thoughts of carp and other species had disappeared through the nearest window.

Talking to a good friend of mine, Adam Whittington, who is an accomplished eel man himself, having caught them intentionally to over 5lb and written about them, we became aware that two 5lb eels in one night is a very rare occurrence and was probably one of the top eel catches of the year. We had to cash in on this and do as much as we could because this could well be a gold mine.

We met at the shop, both clutching a copy of the late John Sidley's book. We armed ourselves with 2oz bombs, 10lb main line; size six and four Super Specialists, a spool of very abrasion resistant 15lb Spiderwire and some beads. We thought this was the right way to go, and from this basic presentation we could ring the changes and alter it as we wished. We decided to fish with light bobbins, line clips and open bail arms. Later on, we changed to the J.S. Eel rig which consisted of 12 inches of 10lb fluorocarbon and six inches of Kryston Supersilk connected via a small swivel, which greatly reduced tangles.

Topper was down there the very next evening, without me (because of my work), and by 12.30am he'd banked his second five of the season at 5lb 1oz. Things were getting serious.

The following night saw both of us at the lake by 7pm, with all rods out on the worm. At about 9.30pm, just as the light was fading, I had my first run at the new lake, resulting in a new PB anguilla at 4lb 2oz and also a PB tench of 7lb 12oz; not a bad brace! No eels to Topper, but his consolation after changing to Icelandic Red boilies at dawn were three tench of 6lb, 6lb 9oz and 7lb 14oz. He also lost a huge tinca that must have been a double - at first we thought it was a carp! It should be noted that we didn't bait up at all; we simply cast solitary double lobworm hookbaits out about 30 yards. I also had a pike of about 7lb just as I was about to pack up. The pike became a bit of a nuisance, as did the grebes; they could see the worms in the clear water and they were nesting at the time, so were on the lookout for anything with which to feed their young.

Topper had the bit between his teeth now and knowing that good things never last, he made it down the next night. Fishing lobworms behind the island, a new area once more saw him finally connect with an eel after missing numerous runs. This was another big eel, weighing 5lb 3oz. He also noticed that landing this eel and returning it seemed to kill the swim. Was this the same eel that had kept taking his bait, or had it alerted the others once it went back?

May the 14th saw us back on the lake. I would have loved to have been there sooner, but I was quite busy with work commitments at the time, so this was the earliest I could make it. We were also keeping the location of our new venue very quiet. This time we tried a different area of the lake, with me in a little bay with an island at around 60 yards in front of me, and Topper to my right in open water. At 10.15pm I had a belter to my left-hand rod in the bay and was in. Eels have an odd way of fighting. It's very jagged and due to their shape and the way they swim they rarely kite, usually swimming backwards on a straight line. You can't mistake an eel when it's hooked. Anyway, this one was what I had come for. She was a new personal best at 5lb 2oz. This was a right result, as I could only fish till midnight because of a very early start in London the next day. Topper didn't score on the eel front, but had another tench of 6lb 6oz. I was beginning to think he was secretly fishing for them!

I kipped the rest of the night at my girlfriend's house which was only a few miles away, and it was on my way to work. I'd leave my rods in her porch, hide my rucksack and bedchair in the boot of my car and do the silly o'clock journey to cook breakfast and lunch for the guys at the Chiswick B.T. building. I would then go straight to the lake after work, via the girlfriend's house to pick up the rods, not a bad arrangement!

Misty, overcast and damp; my anticipation reaches fever point.

I didn't bank any that night, but missed a couple of belters. Topper had another one, this time at exactly 5lb, his fourth five-pounder in a matter of days. He'd had four eels, all five-pounders, quite amazing.

Our next session was on May 18th. Topper had dragged Munchie along for a bash, on the condition that if he told anyone of our secret snake pit we would remove his testicles and make him wear them as earrings! I fished until midnight that night, again without a touch. Munchie missed a one-toner at just after midnight, and guess what... Topper had another, this time a new PB of 5lb 11oz. Just to prove he was still the 'tench king', he also landed a massive male of 7lb 13oz; one of the biggest eels of the year and probably one of the biggest male tench as well; now that's what I call a brace!

The next night saw us back on the lake, again with Munchie because now that he had seen one of our monster eels he wanted to catch one, and he also fancied a big red-eye too! That night was pure madness! I missed 11 runs and Munchie missed eight! Topper had just one run, landing an eel of 2lb 1oz. The strange thing was that we were all in a line, not 30 yards apart, and Topper was in the middle, work that one out! The only explanation we could come up with for the events that occurred that night is that an eel will continue to take a bait until it is hooked, in much the same way that a pike does.

My parents live in a retirement home near Chichester. At the bottom of their garden is a tiny, crystal-clear tributary of the river Arun. It is known by the residents for its population of small eels which you can almost feed by hand.

They are mostly fed the leftovers of numerous Sunday roasts, so it's meat they prefer as opposed to fish. I have tried to feed them with fish and they never appear, yet about three minutes after chucking in three fingernail-sized pieces of cooked chicken that my mum prepares for her cats, the first one appeared, closely followed by another. These two devoured all the meat present. Within five minutes there were a further five eels on my baited spot, but even though they were too late, they continued to search. They would even dig their heads into the bottom where the chicken had originally been. This behaviour suggests that they can pick up the scent of a food source and find the exact spot, even when the food has long gone. They don't seem to use their eyesight at all during feeding; if they did, they would be able to see that there isn't any food there.

This explains why you can miss an eel run, stick a bait out on roughly the same area, and get action straight away. I now mark my line with a piece of tape, clip up and drop the bait on the same spot every time. This observed feeding behaviour had given me the proof I needed to back up the theories that Topper had come up with. If any of this rings any bells, I'd love to hear about it. Just a thought about those meat-eating eels: they don't have much fish in their diet, because there isn't any. The only other fish I have seen in there is the odd stickleback, one 8oz perch and a couple of 5lb commons (escapees from an estate lake, I'm led to believe). The meat introduced by the residents has become their staple diet and they ignore anything else you chuck at them. Does this mean that it is possible to change an eel's main diet just by introducing a new

food source over a period of time? I guess so, and this could be a great advantage if you kept the chosen bait to yourself!

As a footnote about the eels in my parent's stream, I caught two the other day while free-lining chicken for them. The eels picked up the small pieces of meat, not much bigger than the size eight hook I was using, and started to swim off, just holding the bait right on its edge. As they were barely three feet away, and in the gin-clear water, I could see the bait slowly being engulfed as they were swimming off. The hook wasn't far enough into their mouths to make a hook hold until they had swum about a rod length, some 12 feet or so. Incidentally, both of the eels I caught that day behaved in an identical manner. These eels were only about 14 inches long and, assuming this was normal behaviour, how far would a 5lb eel have to travel to engulf the hook, taking into consideration that my 5lb eel was 43 inches long with a girth of nine inches? Food for thought, answers on a postcard!

Right, where was I? On the 21st May, we turned up at the lake, unpacked the gear and realised that we'd left the lobworms at home! Topper had brought along a couple of sardines that he was going to experiment with. This was now the only bait we had, as we couldn't catch any small perch. We fished small sardine sections on all rods. Topper had two screamers, but didn't connect. Obviously these eels were also fish eaters. Incidentally, they all seemed to be the small-mouth variety, normally dubbed as 'worm feeders'. Does anyone have any scientific evidence that an eel actually changes its head shape, or are they just a slightly different strain? If they do change, is it purely for feeding reasons that they do so?

Adam joined us on the 23rd May, as I'd made a bet with him that he'd beat his personal best eel on his first session at our newly-found superlake! I missed a couple, as usual. Now, Adam's a bit of a rig man. He is also one of the best-thinking anglers that I have met. Adam's rig consisted of roughly the same hooklink that we were using, with a size four hook, but his lead arrangement was markedly differently to ours. Unlike

Topper and me, who were using dumpy pear, carp-style leads, Adam was using an elongated torpedo-type lead with a wire stem covered in heat shrink tubing. Onto this stem he had wedged a cork ball of about 20mm which slowed the descent of the lead through the water, and also kept the lead upright on the lake bottom, keeping the main line above any silt or debris that may catch on it. He used a large plastic loop on the lead instead of a swivel and a large diameter bead, and he was also using heavier leads than us so that they wouldn't move during the take.

Switching tactics at dawn brought its rewards.

Adam is hell-bent on the idea that an eel must not feel any resistance during the run. Because an eel is a predator, the initial slight resistance of the line pulling from the clip shouldn't be a problem, because a dying fish may put up a bit of resistance when being grabbed by a hungry eel; but saying that, clips should still be set as light as possible.

Another thing he showed us was a better way of striking. When a normal upward strike is made, the line cuts up through the water, and the action of the rod bending, coupled with stretchy mono, means that only a very little power can be produced at the hook. Just try it on a playing field. With around 50 yards of line out, hold the line and get your mate to strike. Adam's way was to wind down very quickly, keeping the rod horizontal, and then lunge the rod backwards as if to stab someone behind him. This is a far more direct way of setting the hooks.

Adam also showed us the benefits of an elastic band as a clip. A band can be tied on loosely and when the

It didn't take Adam long to get in on the action.

line is pulled into it, gives very minimal resistance. After Adam's advice about the importance of the eel not feeling anything, I scrapped the use of my bobbins, preferring instead the use of a band and open bail arm. I sometimes use an electronic pike drop-off indicator or heavier carp bobbins tied to the rear banksticks so that they hang under the spools.

Adam proved that his theories held water that night. He had one run and landed it! At 5lb 2oz it was a new PB by an ounce; he still owes me 20 quid, come to think of it! On the opposite bank Topper missed a couple of runs before landing yet another 5lb super-snake, this time weighing 2oz over the magical mark. This was his fifth five; like prawn and Thousand Island dressing, this man was on a roll!

Things began to change after this. We did a further four nights for only a couple of runs between us. We were wondering whether the eels we had caught had simply left the lake and gone elsewhere and taken their mates with them. In the past, at a venue he used to fish, Topper had seen a large number of eels disappearing into the woods after they had left a lake that had suffered an oxygen deficiency due to an algae bloom. This does happen. One well-known angler once stated in print that eels don't leave their water once they are in there. Believe me, if they have to, they will.

June 5th was quite chilly with a low mist. At 1.50am we had simultaneous runs. It was quite strange that after four nights of nothing we would have two runs at exactly the same time. Do eels hunt in packs?

They certainly do in my parent's stream. Back to the plot; Topper missed his, but I landed mine (makes a change!). It was about time I had another one. This one was a new PB at 5lb 7oz. Nothing happened after that, apart from a tench of 6lb 8oz and another bloody pike.

Adam joined us again the next day. Nothing to Topper and I, but Adam proved his theories yet again. One run and one fish later, he was cradling a new personal best eel of 5lb 9oz! He also baited up with a pint of maggots which the eel kindly spewed up all over his mat.

It wasn't until July 28th, after a further eight nights without a take, that the next one came. We caught a few small perch with a whip pole. They were now quite abundant in the margins and we decided to give them a go as deadbaits (we struggled to use livebaits due to the numbers of small pike in the venue). After catching a small pike and having three fast runs that were probably eels, Topper had an unusually slow take at about 2am which turned out to be the biggest eel yet at 5lb 11oz 8drams. We didn't get any shots of this one, due to placing it in a keep-net until first light. It was so lively that it wriggled out of his arms. I tried to jump on it, but it still managed to reach the water; it knew exactly where to go!

We thought we'd found the key; that we had to use fish baits, because of the explosion of small perch, and that maybe they had sussed our worm approach. Five further nights of trying to buy a run on the perch dead baits after that last capture proved futile.

Donut off the mark with a four-pounder.

Things then began to really get tough and just getting a run was proving almost impossible. Some nights saw four different baits being used between us, ranging from bunches of maggots, lobworms and small sections of fish, but it was a live perch that finally saw the next eel landed. It was Topper once again that scored, this time with another of exactly 5lb.

Topper continued for a few weeks after this but most nights he recorded little to show for his efforts and he was wondering if the eels were still present, however his persistence paid off and on the 11th of August he connected with yet another 5lb eel, bringing his total for the campaign to nine over the magical 5lb barrier. It was to be Topper's last eel session for the year and although we tried on numerous occasions the following spring, we never managed to catch another eel from this venue or get a run. Just when we thought we had them sussed, they had the last laugh! Never think you have the upper hand; they are always one step ahead of you.

I don't know whether the eels left the lake or not (they could have as the river Blackwater runs just yards behind the lake and a small connecting stream is easily accessible by eels), or whether they just learned to avoid angler's baits (more likely). Incidentally, we never caught the same eel twice and I never again saw any of the seven eels in my parent's stream after catching just two of them. Could the eels that didn't get caught sense stress or discomfort from the ones that did, and therefore decide to vacate an unsafe environment? Whatever happened, I will never know.

Part of an unforgettable brace.

Thorpe Park

The beginning and the end

When I think about the time I spent fishing the lakes at Thorpe Park in Surrey and look at the photos of this magical place, I relax, smile and wish it had lasted a lifetime; however, what seemed like a decade of exploring this vast expanse of water unfortunately lasted for less than a year.

It all started in August 2001, when due to a misunderstanding between me, angling partner, Steve 'Donut' Ansell, and a young, non-diplomatic bailiff at Tarn Pond, controlled by Farnham Angling Society, we became faced with lengthy bans. Worried that I was going to lose what I loved doing so much, fishing, I needed somewhere to settle and was really concerned that I might be out on a limb. Then the call came through; it was Donut asking if I fancied something new. To be honest, I was up for anything and just wanting to get a line in the water, so when he suggested a night on Thorpe Park I grabbed the opportunity with both hands. Donut mentioned that he was going to fish for carp but knowing that I had an interest in other species felt that it would be worth my while grabbing some bream tackle and groundbait.

The following words are taken from my diary and were written the day after that initial session:

Thorpe Park, Wednesday 22nd August 2001.

Standing next to the anglers' hut, on the concrete gabion shoreline and looking out across Manor Lake, I can only describe feeling completely out of my comfort zone. The lake is vast, rich and clear, like an inland sea, yet with little to go on and with the time pushing before darkness, I felt that the area was good for a social and if any fish graced our nets then this would be a bonus.

Conditions weren't ideal, with an easterly wind, a very warm clear night and a high of 19°. Donut managed to get his rods out by boat to the areas he had been told about, but as it was getting dark I just placed a marker around 100 yards on a clear bottom in 20 feet of water and piled

in loads of hemp, corn and pellet, before casting the rods out and hoping. Around midnight we had a large floating weedbed drift into us making it impossible to fish so had to wait until first light to assess the situation and get the rods back out. Shame this happened, as after 40 minutes of casting out I managed a personal best bream of 7lb 7oz followed quickly by another of 8lb 7oz as well as losing a bigger one. Donut poached my swim taking one of 7lb 14oz, but we were left thinking about what could have been. All the fish came on the rods fished with a single tutti-frutti boilie; the other two had doubles on.

To be honest, if it were not for those couple of bream then I probably wouldn't have persisted in chasing a ticket, but to break a personal best twice on the first night in such awkward conditions got my brain working on exactly what these lakes held. Apart from the occasional Pike Anglers Club (PAC) day out, the lakes were pretty much virgin waters. The only definite information I had was that the adjoining Ski Lake had produced at least one pike over 30lb along with plenty of back-up 20s. The lakes were also rumoured to hold a massive common carp around the 40lb mark, known as Saddle Back, and looking at the names that the syndicate had attracted, then there had to be some truth in the rumours.

If this group of waters were capable of producing pike to over 30lb and carp to 40lb then how big could the bream go, let alone other species such as tench and perch? Although I didn't have a ticket, I took some time to investigate just what the complex consisted of, as I wanted to know exactly what it offered if I were to fork out the cash needed for one.

Excluding the Ski Lake, that runs alongside the M3 and was part of another syndicate, the complex housed four lakes within the theme park: namely, Fleet, Abbey, Manor all of which were over a hundred acres in size, as well as a much smaller lake called Nessie. Abbey Lake is connected to the Ski Lake via a small concrete bridge and although it has a fish net to stop movement of fish, this had been neglected and damaged, so straight away I knew that if the Ski Lake could do a 30lb pike then so could any of the other lakes because they were all connected.

One bank was easily accessible from the road, and on closer inspection, the signs were there to be seen of anglers guesting and I'm sure that it was from here that many a rumour had started. On the opposite bank was part of the theme park and it was here that the restaurant boat was positioned, a landmark well known by pike anglers, albeit only accessible by boat during PAC days.

Apart from its size, Fleet was altogether different, generally much shallower and always carrying colour due to its make-up that seemed more clay-like than gravel, and pretty featureless apart from the beds of reeds surrounding it and the metal bridge that connected it to Manor via a channel.

Manor was without doubt the looker and by far the biggest, with numerous bays, gravel sloping reed-fringed margins, and Pirate

Island which sat in crystal clear waters alive with natural food and rich in weed. The more I found out about the venue and syndicate, the more I fancied a ticket. Not only did the element of the unknown excite me, but also being able to fish without any interference, a factor that rarely presents itself on club waters.

The start of things to come. Personal best of 7lb 7oz.

Getting closer to that double.

Adam Whittington was in charge of the syndicate and it took a while to convince him that I would be an asset. I wasn't interested in carp so I could explore the other species that the venue contained, and that was something that could work to his advantage. If the waters were as prolific as he thought, then other specimen anglers could be added without upsetting the carp boys.

It seemed to take an eternity for my ticket to come through, but my persistent reminder to Adam on how I had openly told him of a good eel water, and one from where he was to catch two eels over 5lb, must have had some effect, as eventually, my ticket fell through the door, albeit in late August.

Rules were simple and consisted of just three: first, a life jacket must be worn when in a boat, the second was that no anglers were allowed in boats during the park's opening hours, and the third rule was to use your common sense and respect other anglers. There were a few areas that were out of bounds; the farm, RMC bank and places that were accessible to the public within the park. Other than that, members were allowed to set up wherever they liked, although many of the areas were only reachable by boat.

Donut had bought a BIC Sportyac boat and as he had allowed me use of this, thought it only fair that I purchased an electric motor, battery and fish-finder. Other items of kit that came in useful were mud feet, rakes and a glass-bottomed bucket, all of which had been left in the angling hut and allowed to be used as long as they were put back as they were found.

Having everything sorted, it was just a matter of keeping a close watch on the weather, picking my days, then heading to Thorpe in the hope that the bream would match the pike and carp rumoured to inhabit the lakes.

My ban from FAS had been sentenced, eighteen months in total, yet although completely gutted at the time it was without a doubt the best thing that has ever happened in my angling career and was a pivotal point in making me the angler I am today, so without bearing any grudges, I must thank everyone that was so harsh on me.

Over the next couple of months, my relationship with Thorpe Park, especially Manor, grew and like a new girlfriend, I just couldn't get enough of her. Strangely, Donut's love affair for the venue wasn't as strong and although he accompanied me on a few further visits, soon drifted back to waters closer to home. Looking back, Donut was a carp angler and at the time of joining the venue he had little time to familiarise himself with the carp population before the winter set in. Every now and again he would come down for a social and during these trips would cast out lobworms as the addiction for eels was still running through his blood and often he caught his desired species. Unfortunately, they weren't of the size he had become accustomed to at Mill Lane and I seem to remember that the best was a few ounces over 3lb.

The swim next to the angling hut continued to produce, so there seemed no point whatsoever in moving to pastures new. Regular baiting to a marker float around 70 yards out in the mouth of the channel with plenty of Vitalin laced with corn and pellets saw the bream shoal turning up like clockwork and it got to the stage that I could predict within five minutes when the first liner would happen.

Adam and his friend Andy would often fish on weekends, over my baited area to the far bank. So instead of the Coke bottle, suspended off a bunch of heavy sea weights, I had to rethink and replace this with another system. What I eventually did was to drop a very heavy lead on to the mark, which had a length of strong mono running through it with a big pike float attached to one end. The other end was taken back to shore where I threaded it up the wire of the gabion bank, making sure that the line was pinned to the lakebed, yet taking care that there was enough spare line to be released and allow the pike float to surface when I needed to bait up, and then pulled down and out of sight when not in use. I never told anyone of this, as I thought they might feel it a little irresponsible, but the marker lasted all summer, right through winter and on the very last day, I pulled it in, kissed it, and smiled!

Corn stacks were fished in conjunction with big method feeders and although this tactic produced loads of bream, a problem was noticed, which was liners, even when back leads were employed. It was a problem that I lived with that summer, reluctant to change due to my results, which were far superior to those ever experienced anywhere else. However, with the cooler months approaching, the bream slowly disappeared into deeper water and my attention turned to other species, pike in particular.

Although we had no restrictions on fishing for pike, I had become accustomed to starting for these from the beginning of October. However, the first trip on Fleet Lake drew a blank, so the next trip was planned with Donut to fish in front of the hut on Manor, but on arrival two anglers had already taken the spot.

Respecting their space, we moved into the channel connecting Manor to Fleet and after casting out an eel section, I found myself struggling to connect the bobbin as a pike had already picked this up. The fish soon dropped the bait but just as darkness fell, I received another take which resulted in a pike of 19lb 4oz, shortly followed by another of 16lb 14oz. This was the beginning of a period that would eventually see a fish that would change my whole outlook on fishing; one that would send my adrenalin into overdrive and produce a feeling that I wanted again and again.

The next trip, an overnight session, provided pike to 21lb 13oz, a new personal best, but it was the loss of a very big pike at dawn which left Donut shaking in his shoes and my mind going into overdrive. During these nights spent pike and eel fishing, we had noticed shoals of small fish moving between Manor and Fleet, fish that were later identified as bleak. This was very strange at the time but we were later informed that the complex had been filled up with water from the River Thames so everything fell into place once known. These shoals of bleak would first move through the channel at dusk, a time that saw numerous runs from pike occur, then return through the channel again at midnight, a period that would once again see more pike action, with dawn a standard feeding time seeing further action.

The loss of that big pike by Donut captured my mind and ignoring the other areas that were now producing pike for other anglers, I decided to focus on the same spot the following week. This time, though, I had decided to pop-up roach deadbaits some 20 inches, straight off the lead, to make them more visual to the pike that were obviously feeding on the migrating fry. It was a tactic that was to repay me with the richest of rewards.

After a biteless night, I rose at first light and decided to twitch each bait a few yards. The first two were easily moved back, but the rod in-close was solid, as if it was stuck in weed, but a slight tap on the rod tip alerted my senses that a pike was on and thinking that this fish may

have swallowed the bait, I immediately struck into what was obviously a very big fish. The fish stayed deep, doing nothing spectacular but as it slowly came toward me, then rose in the water, I knew that the fish Donut had lost the previous week was now attached to my line. The crystal clear waters only heightened my nerves as what slowly swam past me more resembled a crocodile, and then with a flick of its tail, it had the rod bent double and line screaming from the reel.

The fight seemed to last forever, but eventually she tired and allowed me to draw her over the waiting net. I still wasn't quite aware of how big she was, and looking in the net I estimated her at a good 20, but as I tried lifting her she started to grow.

Looking out from the point swim. On the left you can see the marker.

The most important fish I have ever caught, and one that probably will never be beaten.

On the mat I thought she was an upper-20 but as I lifted her on the scales my heart skipped a beat as the needle flew past the 30 mark, finally settling at 31lb 10oz. It was a feeling that I can't describe, one when every hair on the back of my neck stood up and the adrenalin rush almost overwhelmed me, yet at that moment I knew it was a feeling I would never tire of.

With the pike back in the water, I was now in a dilemma as my photography skills had yet to be developed. I called Donut who was lodging with me at the time and he did what all good friends would do in such an event, stuck his foot on the throttle and raced up the M3 during rush hour to do the honours with the camera, and what a job he did! There have been few times when I could say that I have released a fish but wanted to keep hold of it forever, but this was one such occasion, yet she needed to return to her home and we watched as she sank into the weed-fringed margins, a sight we will never forget.

The capture of such a fantastic fish was to catapult me into the world of specimen angling but as

Another angle of the 31lb 10oz pike.

expected after reporting the fish to the angling world, it wasn't long before other pike anglers followed in the hope of catching her, and catch her they did; namely David Seaman and Gary Newman, both times over 32lb, so its comforting to know that my capture did little to harm her.

I continued throughout that winter in the hope of catching another unknown monster but as the temperatures dropped so did my catch rate and apart from the occasional pike to high double it became a gruelling exercise. It's strange when I look back

knowing that at the time I wasn't enjoying things, fishing through extreme cold and on partly frozen lakes, but then you realise that those times were ones of character building, that even in hindsight you wouldn't swap and its those times that made Thorpe Park so special.

Nessie, the smaller lake, was probably my saviour as more often than not I could drop on to it and get a few pike. However, I think the best that came from there was a shade over 20lb, and the best I had was around 16lb.

It was a cruel place in winter.

One morning I will always remember was when I was awoken by a take at first light on a popped-up natural. The strike was met with a strange feeling transmitted down the rod blank, and then in the distant mist I saw a cormorant surface, shaking its head. At this point, the surface erupted with dozens of them, some with fish, mainly perch, in their beaks, many of which were dropped all around me as they took off in fright. The problem I had was that I was playing an angry bird that was coming ever closer, but, just as I was contemplating hitting it with the landing net handle the hooks pulled and it flew skyward.

Nessie was also a great place to grab a few livebaits and it was here that Donut and I stumbled on an outlet that was full of fish. Once again, the water was crystal clear, and looking into its depths to an area that was no bigger that the roof of a car we could see some sizeable roach. Pike were momentarily forgotten and eventually, through the numerous, ruffe, bleak, skimmers, perch and small roach, the odd better fish was landed with Donut catching the best, a roach we estimated at over 2lb.

The harsh winter finally passed and with the coming of April the lakes started to liven up. It was a time that saw me and my father spending numerous hours afloat in the small boat looking through a glass-bottomed bucket at features below, and the echo sounder allowed us to understand the topography of these underwater giant gravel pits. We visited the venue maybe three times a week, sometimes to fish but always to bait a couple of marks, one in Fleet, the other in Manor, and it wasn't long before the bream revisited the warmer shallows, especially within Fleet.

One session I remember well was in mid-April while bream fishing in Fleet. I was continuously receiving line bites which saw the indicator rise to the rod blank and hang there for a couple of seconds before dropping back. I remembered watching pike in the margins on another lake causing the same line bites so I headed for the nearest shop, bought some sardines and returned. After flicking one out no more than two rod lengths from the bank, the first run came in the shape of a 15lb 5oz pike quickly followed by a further ten which included pike of 17lb 4oz, 17lb 6oz,

18lb 13oz and 19lb 15oz, before they exhausted me of bait. As I packed up, I called an angler who I had become friends with over the winter, Russell from Chertsey, and told him to get down as the pike were going mad. Get down he did, taking time of work, but in the same swim, fishing four rods, just hours later, he failed to get a bite - that's fishing!

It was later that month, a time in my life when the stresses and strains were few and I could simply disappear on a Sunday afternoon with the view of

The biggest of four that totalled a staggering 84lb!

Slightly bigger than the club waters!

fishing right through until Tuesday morning, and it was probably these sessions that I remember the most and made the experience so special. The standard spaghetti Bolognese and bottle of red wine would be taken, and after baiting up, I would sit back, eat a good warm meal cooked in the fishing hut and then slowly enjoy the effects of a couple of glasses of wine which would only heighten my expectations of that longed-for 10lb bream, the fish that I had joined the syndicate for in the first place.

The 20th of April saw one such session and bathed in glorious sunshine I was all set by 5pm, two rods on the standard, critically-balanced corn, fished in conjunction with 2oz inline leads, one on a boilie slightly off the baited area and the fourth rod offering a sardine, in the mouth of the channel.

The reason for changing from method feeders to inline leads was to cut down the problem of liners. Where I had been baiting was on a slope and as the bream feed around the feeders they would roll, something that inline leads didn't do. Looking back, I thought that the 'method lead' had been discovered while barbel fishing on the Loddon, but I now know that it was only developed further.

When it started taking line under the rod tip, I knew it wasn't a bream!

All was quiet until dusk, but then the liners started and come dawn, nine bream had fallen, the best a shade over 9lb. I hooked a fish at dawn, though, which made me realise that we should always expect the unexpected. The 'bream' under the rod tip started to take line and then, as it exploded on to the surface, I saw the bronze flank of a barbel – yes, a barbel – that weighed 5lb 11oz.

The temperature rose to 22° that day, comfortable enough for some shut-eye and come the time the theme park's rides started and screaming kids could be heard

in the distance, I was in the land of Nod. I had become accustomed to expect that if a run developed during the hours of daylight, ignoring the first two hours of light, then it would be from a tench and that day two 6-pounders awoke me.

Russell arrived the following evening and wanted to fish the channel entrance and as the pike rod hadn't received any enquiries I was happy to move it to my left. It was on moving this rod that the session became a real red-letter one, as soon after casting out, a run developed that produced another special fish in the form of a pike weighing 25lb 2oz. Repositioning the rod, I couldn't set the bobbin as a pike of 22lb 6oz had picked up the sardine, and I lost another big fish from a hook-pull moments later.

Russell had borrowed Donut's boat and tied it to the gabion cage but obviously his knots needed some attention as I noticed something was missing; the boat! With 300 acres of water in front of us, I didn't hold out too much hope for him as he headed into the darkness in search of the boat, however, some 20 minutes later he redeemed himself by returning, boat in tow, and as he did so was welcomed by me, bent into a pike on his rods, one that he took over and landed weighing 20lb 10oz. After his catch we sat stunned at what we had just caught, enjoyed a glass of wine and soon were snoring our heads off, glad that the bream were in an uncooperative mood. At first light, my pike rod was away again and on landing a fish of 15lb14oz, I realised that we had just taken four pike for a total weight of 84lb. What a night!

The reason for cramming two-nighters in was that there were rumours that the fishing syndicate was to cease come June 15th. I wanted to make sure that if such an event occurred I could safely say that I had given the venue my best shot.

May arrived and the pike rod was still producing, the best a repeat of the 22lb 6oz fish, this time down in weight, probably from spawning, at 21lb 4oz, yet just around the corner, the tench were waking up and another surprise was waiting. The bream continued to grace my net throughout the month, but the

commonplace 11-pounders reported by the carp anglers were noticeable by their absence.

Another species that was now making a regular appearance was roach/bream hybrids. These looked more like roach than bream and often a heartbeat was missed as a specimen slid across the drawstring before the bream factor kicked in.

After all the hard work raking, baiting and placing the marker Chris brings it in on his first cast!

What a fish and the sun shines once again for the photos. I class this fish almost as good as the pike; a fish of a lifetime and one I may never better.

If this had been a roach I would have become famous. A roach bream hybrid and personal best weighing 5lb 15oz.

Monday the 27th of April was the next highlight of my Thorpe adventure. There was no apparent reason why the bream rods had been slow during the night but at dawn one of the corn rods ripped off and after a spirited fight a huge tench weighing 9lb 10oz dropped into the net. How I would have loved to have landed the one that followed just five minutes later, but it wasn't to be and it is such fish that are seen and lost that keep me coming back for more. Was it a double? Oh yes, it was massive!

June arrived and it became common knowledge that the syndicate was to end. Adam had tried his hardest to keep it going but due to health and safety regulations it wasn't to be. Manor Lake had been very kind to me and having angling friends that were still fishing on club waters, I decided that I would take them as guests, so they too could enjoy what Thorpe had to offer.

Chris Charlton was the first, and after the standard baiting-up routine had been completed, he cast out, only to get caught up with my carefully placed marker. We fished the night under the stars, it was one of those clear nights when the sky is just ablaze with them and come morning he had managed to land a personal best bream. However, after open-airing it, he paid the price and spent the following week in bed after catching a chill. Both my dad and brother spent the odd night on Thorpe's magical banks, catching plenty of bream with Kevin landing a pike of 20lb 12oz, yet there was still more to come.

Having just a couple of weeks to go, I threw everything I could at the place, taking numerous bream, not the double, but a roach-bream hybrid of 5lb 15oz, plus a carp of 13lb 13oz put in an appearance. Then, on the final night, June the 14th, another magnificent fish dropped into my net. It was another superb pike and the last fish to grace my net on this magical place, weighing 24lb 2oz. It was the perfect way to end a chapter in my angling career. Thorpe will be dearly missed, and never forgotten.

A fitting end to an incredible place.

France

This was to be my first fishing holiday abroad and the thought of relaxing in warm sunshine, drinking red wine and catching plenty of carp was really exciting. Donut, my angling companion, had fished the famous Lake Cassien on a couple of occasions so it was left to him to tap into his angling contacts in regard to the venues we would fish.

A big lake, well down south, called Beaumont de Lomagne was the one he most wanted to visit as it had been producing some mighty carp in excess of 50lb. We were also fortunate as just an hour from the venue lived some relations of Donut's, and both were anglers so we made the decision to make our way down to them for the middle part of the holiday.

At the time we were both field testers for Nashbait and had ordered around 50 kilos of Monster Pursuit to take with us. However, just before we were due to leave, the country was hit with an outbreak of foot and mouth and the authorities had put a restriction on the movement of any products containing fishmeal. This included boilies, but having no contacts in France, the decision was made to stash them out of sight, in every available space, and hope that we wouldn't get stopped through customs. I don't know what the implications would have been had we had been caught, but we nervously boarded the ferry. How we got through the French Custom Control is anyone's guess because Steve's Mondeo was seriously overweight and we both cringed as we slowly made our way down the ramp and off the ferry, fully expecting the car to bottom out and heads to turn, but luck was with us and we sailed straight through.

We were hoping to find the night fishing zone on the river Mayenne around Grez-Neuville, but this seemed impossible to locate and as we had already chanced our luck with customs, we felt it sensible not to chance it with the local gendarmerie who took night fishing in the wrong areas very seriously, and decided to park up and catch up on some well-needed sleep. Apart from Pink Floyd, Steve's taste of music is somewhat contrasting to mine, however we had agreed that each would be allowed to play a tape in turn throughout the journey. Knowing he was well into Eminem at the time, an artist I just couldn't stand and knowing he was going to be playing this as often as possible, I created a game plan and bought a Celine Dion tape along that would be played

36lb 13oz catfish. Now where's that cigar!

Our rods ripped off together.

after this. It didn't take long for a truce to be called and we agreed not to play these any more, but I do remember listening to some of the lyric, of how Eminem was going to cut his mother's throat, and as I drifted off for the night I recall placing my hand over my throat, I felt that disturbed!

The following morning, we found the local tackle shop in Angers and they kindly pointed us in the direction of a day-ticket water called La Grande Maison in the small village of Cheffes. At just £7 a night and with onsite toilets, showers and tackle shop, as well as the chance of a 60lb-plus sturgeon, 50lb catfish and 30lb carp, it sounded perfect.

The lake was around 20 acres and there was no one in the onsite shop when we arrived, so we simply parked up and walked out on to a peninsular to view the lake. There were a couple of French anglers on the far bank but as we stood looking across the lake, carp after carp launched themselves in front of us at around 60 yards. The main body of the lake was to our right but with the wind pushing to our left, it was obvious that this was the prime position to be in, and once the owner arrived back, and after considerable convincing, he allowed us to set up in these swims. We could only fish them for two nights, due to a local school using the amenities, but with loads of fish in front of the swims, two nights was more than enough.

My best from La Grande Maison.

Donut took the left-hand side as he fancied the margin in the bay, leaving me content with just launching my rigs to the showing fish. He had brought along a big Cuban Cohiba cigar and an expensive bottle of port which he placed on a small table between the swims. The cigar was the prize for the first fish, and the port a celebration for both on its capture. After setting up, he blew the whistle and out went the rigs.

Ten minutes later, I was puffing away on the cigar, sipping a glass of port but also soaking wet as prior to Donut throwing me in the lake, I had just done battle with a personal best catfish of 36lb 13oz. It was a great start to the holiday and with the weather forecast looking good and a couple of modest carp falling that evening we settled down for our first night.

Sunset on Beaumont.

Donut was a chef at the time and also writing for Carp Talk, producing the very well-received article called 'Bivvy Cuisine'. This was an added bonus as he was always willing to cook; all I had to do was to take some photos as well as consume whatever he created and on that first night it was a plateful of giant garlic prawns.

The fishing that first night was amazingly quiet, with just one fish falling to my rods and again, another cat, this time weighing 22lb 6oz. However, as dawn broke the carp became active and throughout the day we received steady action with a total of 16 carp being landed.

As darkness fell, the carp once again stopped feeding leaving the cats to feed and although Donut never caught one, my rods ripped off twice in the night producing cats of 30lb 11oz and 11lb 8oz. As dawn broke the carp started to feed again and by the time we had to move from the area we had taken a total of 36 fish between us, with the best carp weighing 23lb 12oz, 25lb 10oz and 26lb 9oz.

The lake has a system where you are told where to fish, hence the reason for struggling to convince the owner to allow us to fish the point swim when we arrived, yet after packing away late that evening and not wanting to travel through the night, we accepted a couple of new swims at the opposite end of the lake. These had the wind off our backs and knowing the fish were at the other end of the lake, unsurprisingly, we blanked.

God knows what the French ladies made of us!

Rob cooking us Toulouse sausage.

After a hearty breakfast we were back on the road heading south to Donut's relatives that were based at Saint-Matre. The journey was long, upwards of 11 hours, but we finally arrived in the early hours and were thankful of a comfortable bed for the night.

The following day we fished a local lake, rumoured to have carp to over 40lb, but apart from a few small commons that drifted past in the margins, and after much looking, nothing remotely near this showed, so we headed back to the gîte, and prepared everything for Beaumont the next day.

Rob and Tim joined us for the first night on Beaumont and, on arrival, things looked good as not only did we have some 60 acres of water to ourselves, but carp could be seen crashing at distance, albeit well out of casting range.

Rob cooked the evening meal consisting of lamb and Toulouse sausage, and once again the red wine flowed and although the rods remained silent, there was plenty to look at, namely fit female joggers! Apart from Tim missing a run, the night passed uneventfully and come the morning Tim and Rob departed.

We had two more nights ahead of us and fish were showing in front of our swims, but our baits were being stolen by crayfish so we created a plan; using a throwing stick, we would send a kilo of bait out every hour. This would keep the swim topped up and we hoped it would draw a few fish into casting range, but with daytime temperatures reaching 44° and night-time dropping to just 10°, this became an energy-sapping procedure.

However, it was a plan that worked and, slowly but surely, fish started to show over our baits around 100 yards out, and over the next 48 hours we landed 33 carp, the best a disappointing 26lb 1oz. I say disappointing because we were expecting the carp to be far bigger, and when news came through that two Belgian anglers had caught 16 fish from outside their huts on the far bank, over a week's fishing, which including five 30s, we knew that we had either been in the wrong place or just been very unlucky.

After our successful session on Beaumont, we once again met up with Tim and Rob, this time heading to a dammed area of the River Lot at Cabanac, but on arrival we found that the water level was extremely low. Although we had 48 hours at our disposal, we only fished for 24 as it became obvious that something wasn't quite right, and with no bites or sightings of carp we called it a day.

The carp still fed in the heat of the day.

Scrapper twenty.

Our biggest from Beaumont, 26lb 1oz.

My best from Beaumont, exactly 24lb.

Tim mentioned another area called 'The Field of Water' at Moissac and this is where we headed next, yet we never felt completely comfortable here as it was a meeting point for lots of youngsters and apart from a small catfish, and sitting out an amazing electric storm, we were happy to pack up and move to a section of the River Tarn at Le Soulas the following morning.

We managed ten commons on that last night, the best going 16lb 14oz and it was noticeable that these fish wanted tiger nuts. They were amazingly powerful, all torpedo-shaped and truly wild, and if I had lost the first fish, would have put money on it being a thirty! It was also a dangerous place to be. When we arrived, the river was some four feet down and the exposed river bed was slippery and very muddy. The water level fell a further two feet in the evening, treacherous conditions for landing a fish, and when it rose five feet in the night, we really did feel vulnerable.

After an eventful last night in France we headed north toward Cherbourg, a journey of some 13 hours. We were tired and touchy, and after getting lost in downtown Cherbourg in the early hours, we found ourselves throwing all the toys out of the pram. I'm not too sure what it was all about but after arguing for a few seconds we realised that the surrounding area looked somewhat dodgy, and with flat lights being turned on, dogs barking and the odd disturbed Frenchman shouting a load of abuse at us, we decided it was better to get in the car and locate the ferry!

Having to cool down with this 25lb common.

A place to settle
Petersfield Heath

When the Thorpe Park syndicate finished, and being unable to fish Farnham AS waters due to being banned, I thought that I would be at a loose end during the summer of 2002. However, once again, it was Blobby who came to the rescue and suggested that I tried Petersfield Boating Lake for eels. He mentioned rumours of a ten-pounder being caught accidentally a few years before, and had himself taken a five-pounder the previous winter on a bait intended for pike.

81

I also found out that Adrian Eves had fished the lake for eels over a number of years, during which time he had taken them to well over 6lb. Tapping him up for some information, he mentioned that he thought the lake was past its best and was thinking about moving on. It was then that I mentioned Mill Lane on the Farnham ticket and being unable to fish the water myself thought it would be the ideal water for him to try out. We ended the conversation joking that if we swapped venues we might go on to land monsters. Little did we know!

It was on the 23rd June 2002 that I found myself settled on the banks of the Boating Lake. That first night could well have been the last as I was tucked away in a tight swim, well out of view of onlookers, as travellers had somehow breached the barriers on one bank. Just like any first night on a new water, expectations weren't high. All I wanted was to learn slowly about how the water ticked, prepare kit and make notes as I went, so that eventually, tactics, bait and location would fall into place.

Lobworms were placed on one rod and after hearing reports of eels picking up pike baits, and due to having no fresh naturals, I placed a section of sardine on the other. The first lesson learned was that if worms were going to be used, they would have to be fished in the margins as the lake was full of greedy bream that kept me awake most of the night, not what I wanted when I was trying to keep a low profile. The sardine section stayed quiet all night, but just as the light was increasing, a fast run on this saw me striking thin air and although this could well have been a pike, it was enough to get my thoughts racing and just three days later I was back.

The travellers had moved on, so I decided to set up on the golf course bank which was far more comfortable. Both rods were baited with lobworms and placed in the margins. At 11.35pm, I watched as after a couple of audible indications the line pulled from the clip and with mono pouring from the spool sensed that the culprit had to be an eel.

Engaging the bail arm, I swept the rod back only to find it almost being ripped out of my hands. Luckily the clutch was set and instantly, I knew that a big eel had been hooked by the way it shook its head then took line. A jelly-leg moment then commenced as I struggled to get what was obviously a very big eel into the landing net. However this was achieved eventually and when I looked down I knew that I had found a place to settle as this had to be a five-pounder.

I wish I had done some self-takes, but a couple were having a romantic stroll around the lake and had stopped, so I asked if they could take a few pictures for me. Although they came out, you could hardly see me in it, but the entire 18th hole was visible in the background. It was an incredible start. The eel weighed 5lb 2oz and later became part of a brace, with another weighing 3lb 4oz.

The next two visits saw the true potential of the water become clear as fishing a different swim I managed another two eels weighing 4lb 4oz and 4lb 8oz. However, a two-week angling holiday in France brought my eel sessions to an abrupt end. All the time I was away, I couldn't help but think that another eel goldmine had been discovered and although the experience of angling abroad was great, I couldn't wait to get home and reacquaint myself with the Boating Lake.

The next two nights, though, were an anticlimax, as although runs were encountered, all were missed, yet late in July I managed to land another brace, these weighed 4lb 3oz and 4lb 5oz. However, things could have been far better as I missed at least six other runs. One thing that I have always tried to do is to keep on the move when eel fishing, never exhausting one swim, as eels soon wise up and by fishing different areas you

can often stay a step ahead of them and catch a few more than by becoming static.

Donut, also an eel fanatic, had joined me by now. He was missing runs too, but finally managed to connect and land his first eel from the venue, one weighing exactly 4lb, early in August, a night that I also landed one of 4lb 11oz. Another four, this time 4lb 10oz, followed on the next night session, one that showed a distinct mark on its head in the shape of a jet black diamond.

What an incredible fish! Personal best eel of 7lb 1oz 8drams.

I had been interested in an article in one of the weeklies mentioning that there was very little evidence of an eel being caught twice and the author mentioned that he felt they either died or left the water. I found this difficult to believe, as how can you identify an eel? So, from that capture I started to take close-up photographs of any small mark on an eel's body, including the black diamond. I'm glad I did as the following year this eel once again graced my net, caught on the same bait at the same weight, in fact I caught it three times in three years!

A couple of frustrating nights followed, when numerous runs were missed on both the worms and fish sections,

before the next capture. This time it was an eel weighing 3lb 11oz, yet it was the surprise visit to the bank of two upper-double common carp on rudd heads that shocked me.

Our eel sessions saw us trying other new waters and one night Donut and I settled on one of the Hollybush pits run by Farnborough Angling Club. I knew the lake contained eels as, once again, I'd been told of a pike angler catching a fairly big eel while pike fishing.

After settling in a swim, the bites soon came, not from eels but mosquitoes and I remember saying this was the

An early brace of fours taken from Petersfield Heath.

The biggest of five taken in one night, 6lb 7oz.

first and last night I would be found here, yet this was soon forgotten once the eels became active. Once again, we both missed numerous bites before landing an eel each, mine weighed 3lb 11oz and Donut's 2lb 9oz, not as big as the Boating Lake, but still worth a another night sometime in the future.

My most memorable catch on the Boating Lake was late in August. It was a night when I nearly didn't bother, as on arrival I found loads of kids celebrating their end-of-term exams results. Radios were blaring, kids were running, dancing and throwing up everywhere, many obviously well under the influence, and when the bottles started to be thrown in the lake and beer cans came floating past I questioned my sanity. Around midnight a thick, eerie, damp

mist descended on the lake, the kids disappeared and the carp started launching themselves out of the water.

Here are the actual words taken from my diary:

Petersfield Heath, Thursday 23rd August.
Arriving at 6.30pm I wanted to fish around peg 20 but with anglers here and also on the boards, reluctantly dropped into peg 27 again. This swim has produced runs in the past, but all have been missed. Tried to catch some small fish but this proved difficult only managing two rudd and a skimmer along with half a dozen bream that were far too big to use. Nearly came home as there wasn't any movement and felt it was going to be a hard night, along with the kids celebrating their exam results. Thank God I didn't!

Together they weighed 11lb 9oz.

No action until midnight, so changed the rudd head to the skimmer's head as the bigger bait might induce a run, this it did and around 2am I received a dropped run. At 3am the rod fishing the rudd tails just melted away, contact made and a 4lb 10oz eel graced my net. Well happy as it was far more than I'd expected so cast the rod back out and dozed off. Another aborted run on the rudd head woke me in the early hours, then at first light around 6am, far later than normal due to the thick fog, my left-hand rod on the skimmer's head ripped off. What happened next I will never forget.

Contact made and the fish moved to the left, side strain turned it and it moved to the right. Until now it felt different,

a bit between a pike and an eel. Halfway in, the lead's spotted and by the way the line was moving from side to side it was definitely an eel. The head came up next to the rushes, it was huge, but just how big? In the net first time and I was shaking; target hit, a six I hoped. She was much lighter in colour than the others, almost an olive green and livelier with one of her pectoral fins showing a bite mark and the other almost missing. I will know her again if caught. Eventually, in the sling she went, 7lb 1oz 8drams. I was speechless. Blobby was called and duly hurried down to do the honours with the camera; they'd better be good! Anglers Mail called and it looks like this is the biggest eel of the year caught by design. She measured 44 inches in length and has a girth of 11 inches!

After that eventful night things toughened up. Ten more sessions were crammed in during the month of September for two 4lb eels. At first, I was still getting runs but even these dried up and come the end of the month it was obviously time to move on.

During this period, Adrian Eves returned. We had kept each other up to date of our catches; however, Adrian was eager to tell me that all his hard work throughout the summer at Mill Lane hadn't gone to waste, as he too had finally landed his dream fish, a 7lb eel. Just to prove how good he is, he landed an eel of 5lb 12oz that night! With autumn setting in and seeing results drop off, it was time to move on and with perch and barbel captivating my mind, the eels on the Boating Lake were left alone.

The spring of 2003 finally arrived and with the weather unseasonably warm I found myself back on Petersfield Heath far earlier than expected, March 25th to be precise. Nothing happened that first evening but just two nights later, my first eel of the campaign was caught, albeit the smallest I ever took from the water, weighing just 2lb 8oz.

Information of another potential eel water on the south coast came in, this time from Simon Scott at Sparsholt College who had been electro-fishing the water and seen two huge eels surface. The venue also contained some big bream and although I fished the venue on numerous occasions, always found myself caught between these and the eels.

Donut at last gets off the mark with this four.

Dawn on a new venue.

This was confused further one morning when I watched as a massive tench, estimated at around 12lb, came waddling past. Looking back now, I kick myself for not concentrating on the eels, and finding myself caught in two minds was probably the reason my results were appalling, as I never caught an eel, a bream or a tench from at least half a dozen nights during the month of April. The Heath was also proving difficult and apart from Donut catching a four-pounder, come early June, I had failed to get on the score sheet. However, this run of form was just about to end in dramatic fashion.

Here are the words taken from my diary;

Petersfield Heath, Thursday 5th June.

Golden balls does it again! Fished the Swings swim with Donut, an area that for some reason I'm not that keen on.

The night was clear, calm and a little chilly, conditions that have produced here before. First run came at 10.00pm which resulted in an eel of 5lb 9oz followed by a missed run at 11pm on a tail section. At midnight, two runs almost simultaneously resulted in eels of 3lb 12oz and 6lb 1oz along with two more runs at first light which produced an eel of 4lb 15oz! Donut missed two runs, probably due to using baitrunners. The 5lb 9oz eel showed an unmistakable mark on its side, one that has been photographed and filed. I must admit my heart hasn't

really been into eel fishing of late but it's well and truly rekindled now.

Three days later, I was back, still on a high from the last session and having had such a manic night in the Swings swim, I broke a long-standing tradition and dropped back into the same swim. Eighteen runs came that night, once again starting at around 10pm and come the morning five eels were being photographed. These eels weighed 4lb 4oz, 4lb 7oz, 4lb 10oz, 5lb 11oz and another monster at 6lb 7oz. It was a remarkable couple of nights, one that I have never repeated, and was the nail in the coffin for Donut as he left that morning with his tail securely tucked between his legs, as over the course of two seasons he had only taken two 4lb eels, a statistic that just goes to prove that some venues are kind to you and others are cruel and for Donut, the Boating Lake was cruel.

This mark proved that I caught this eel twice.

When we talk about Petersfield Heath, I always mention Stillwater to Donut, as one summer we carp fished together, often side by side using identical tactics and bait. I caught two carp that summer while Donut caught around 20, including most of the big ones. The capture of those nine eels also proved something else; eels do get recaptured as the 4lb 10oz eel had a distinct black diamond on its head, one that matched my photograph taken the previous summer.

Five further sessions saw just two, three-pounders taken before the next memorable night which fell on July 1st. My time on the Heath showed that the most productive nights usually fell on clear calm nights, often with a full moon, but tonight was the complete opposite, wet and stormy. I wasn't that confident to be honest and headed to a new swim that had only recently been opened in another corner of the lake. 10pm came and with it the first run on a rudd head and as the rod hooped over I felt that I might just be in for another historic catch; however, the culprit was the first of three common carp that came before midnight. Things then went quiet for a couple of hours before four runs saw me striking thin air. Fortunately, the next two runs were converted and come first light, eels weighing 5lb 7oz and 6lb 2oz were being photographed, and once again marks on the smaller of the two showed a mark that matched one from the previous year.

Half a dozen further trips produced just one 3lb eel and come September, I was about to call it a day, but a couple of eels in my fish tank in the living room suddenly came to life and became so active that I just had to grab the tackle for one last go. Setting up under the trees in the outlet corner, two runs came resulting in a 4lb 10oz eel.

For some reason, my first session of 2004 wasn't until April 28th. This night, a blank was recorded, a result that started to become common. It was also a time when some distressing news filtered through that a number of big eels had been found the previous winter with their heads missing. I tried to investigate further, to find out the reason this was happening and just how many had fallen to this fate, yet little was gained.

I knew the information was true as there was a local woman who fed the ducks every morning, religiously. She wasn't that keen on anglers but over the previous couple of seasons had come to realise that I respected everything around me and would pick up litter and discarded line that less concerned anglers had left on the bank, and with her confirming these dead eels, I felt somewhat sickened.

I still cannot believe that anglers were to blame. The more obvious answer would be otters, yet back in 2004 otter sightings anywhere in this part of the county were rare and to think that they would be hunting in such a rural area is just as difficult to comprehend. What actually happened will never be known, but my eel captures that summer were poor. Runs were hard to come by and just three were caught, the best 4lb 8oz and come September, I decided to move on with the intention of not returning for a number of years.

Unfortunately, the venue was to suffer another devastating blow, as an algae bloom the following year saw the oxygen level being depleted and as a result the venue lost a very high percentage of its stock. The following year another algae bloom produced similar results and with few, if any, fish remaining the club decided not to renew its lease from the council.

Whether or not all the eels survived is unknown, but I doubt it. However, a picture last season showed that they weren't completely wiped out as a youngster was spotted in one of the angling weeklies holding up a good eel, probably a four, caught during the day on a boilie. Donut and I did spend an emotional night on the water on June 16th 2010 in the hope that the eels were still a viable target, but come the morning, the indicators had failed to move and we left feeling that another eel paradise had been lost.

Although I have read the late John Sidley's book on eel fishing on numerous occasions, and brought many of his tactics into my eel fishing, I overlooked one vital piece of information, this being that many of his biggest eels had been caught during daylight through the winter.

Part of an historic catch of nine specimen eels over two nights.

It's something that I should have responded to, as just like roach switch from being nocturnal feeders in the autumn and early winter, come the New Year, when the water temperature is at its lowest, they seem to switch to feeding in the daylight. Knowing that a few big eels had been caught by pike anglers during the winter months, it's about the only thing that I regret not testing out on the Boating Lake, but it's too late now.

Since those three long summer campaigns on Petersfield Heath, my quest for an eel to beat my personal best has taken me to numerous waters and although I have never fished as hard as I did on the Boating Lake, each season a number of nights are spent targeting this fascinating species.

Without a doubt, the most rewarding capture since the monster from Petersfield Heath is that of a 6lb 9oz eel caught from a stretch of the river Loddon in July 2008. My brother and father were fishing the river and I had taken a couple of hours out to visit them. A couple of other anglers had settled further upstream so I

Another six from the boating lake that showed a distinctive mark on its side.

wandered up for a chat. While talking, one of the angler's rods pulled over and he struck into what he first thought was a chub. The fish then started taking line and I said that it must be a barbel, however a few minutes later a massive eel surfaced. To say I was astonished is an understatement, but it was that big, and I watched as his friend tried to get it into a smallish pan landing net. The pole was bent over double and I expected to hear a loud crack as it shattered but a few feet from the water the eel launched itself skyward, breaking his hooklink and disappearing. I couldn't believe what I had just seen.

Two days later, I set up for the night further downstream in an area of deep, sluggish water. A few bleak were caught for bait and after casting the rods out, one baited with a fish section the other with worms, I sat back and enjoyed watching a barn owl hunt in the adjacent field. Around 1am, the worm rod flew into action and the alarm screamed. I'm almost expecting a barbel but straight away I knew It was an eel and after a hard fight managed to get the huge fish into the net. It's often the case that if you catch one eel, then another will follow and in the early hours another turned up, this time weighing 4lb 5oz.

The last eel I caught from the Heath.

A self-take at Frensham Great Pond.

Other venues that I have tried include Frensham Great Pond and Lakeside in Eastleigh, a water well known for its big eels which are usually taken accidentally by carp anglers. Again, it was Simon Scott who forwarded this information and I remember numerous sleepless nights spent targeting the eels. I don't like being beaten by a lake, especially when eels are my target, yet this venue did just that. It wasn't that I didn't catch eels, I did, the best a shade under 4lb, but it was my conversion rate that was abysmal. Every night as darkness fell, the bites would start. I tried every rig and every bait, yet it didn't make a difference and I would say that one in a dozen runs was hooked. The final straw came when one night I received no sleep, as no fewer than 28 runs were encountered, yet not one eel was hooked! I left that morning, hot, sweaty and completely knackered, and muttering more than a few choice words.

Frensham Great Pond is totally different to Lakeside. If you get a bite you're lucky, but I've had a high percentage of bites hooked and landed. It's what I would classify as a very hard eel water as I feel there are very few eels in the 60-odd acres, an estimate that's reinforced by the number of them that are accidentally caught. I know of two, and if you consider the amount of maggots that are emptied into the lake each year by tench and rudd anglers, I feel privileged to have taken around eight eels from the venue, the best going 6lb 11oz.

As I complete this chapter I'm smiling because a CEMEX Angling Gold Card has just dropped through my letterbox, something I never expected to receive due to the venues being sold, and something that I have been wanting to do for a long time is to fish Horton Church Lake for eels, a session that will certainly happen this summer.

This 5lb 13oz eel was caught accidentally whilst fishing for catfish.

Perch paradise

Kingfisher (Teddington Weir)

A perch campaign on the River Thames at Teddington Weir in 2002 was well under way, and having taken them to over 3lb in our first few trips, it seemed that this would be where Blobby and I would settle, especially when news filtered through that it had just produced a brace weighing 3lb 11oz and 4lb 11oz.

I had been introduced to the river a few years prior to this and up to now only taken tentative steps to explore this great weir, for it was a venue that I didn't look forward to fishing. It wasn't due to what the venue had to offer, but the problems surrounding fishing there. One of the headaches was the journey up the M3. It was a nightmare because they were widening the lanes, which created long tailbacks even in the early hours. Another frustrating factor was that the perch seemed to prefer livebaits and although catching these wasn't a problem, it swallowed up valuable time at dawn, which is probably the best perch feeding spell of them all.

The parking around the weir was also a nightmare, so most trips started very early in the morning, and if I left it too late, I often found myself parking miles away and having a long walk to get to the river. Couple all these problems with a section of the Thames that is tidal, as well as being popular with some of the best perch anglers in the country, and you can see why my love for the venue never really blossomed.

This wasn't the only drawback, as even when I did get everything right and found myself in one of the better areas, if the weather turned bad, trying to erect an umbrella on the shingle or concrete bank often proved nigh on impossible. I always tried to fish the weir in overcast conditions as perch fishing is far better then, but more often than not it rained, and I found myself holding an umbrella pole so it didn't get blown away - far from ideal. This problem was overcome by purchasing some good waterproofs, but the bites at Teddington seemed to come in short bursts, probably due to the tide, and sitting in torrential rain, sometimes for hours, knocked much of the enjoyment out of the sessions.

I remember the last session I ever did at Teddington for two reasons. I was fishing on the far bank, just downstream of the blue footbridge and standing out in the river, wearing chest waders, on what looked like it could turn into a red-letter day. A stock of bleak livebaits had been caught at first light and the river ran with a lovely green tinge to it. Anglers were noticeable by their absence and with Blobby to the left of the slipway, I trotted the small bleak downstream alongside the boat mooring platform.

Every trot down saw the float dip, then slide away toward the platform and numerous perch to well over 2lb graced my net. I was in my element, as I had longed for this day when all the pieces of the jigsaw came together and as the float buried once again, I watched as line left the clutch. Finally, a big perch slid over the net and like a child in a sweet shop, I ran across the footbridge cradling this perch in my landing net to show Blobby. The perch weighed 3lb 4oz 8drams, by far my biggest Thames perch, and after a quick photo found myself once again locked in battle with another three-pounder. I knew that I was on to a winner and that if things stayed as they did then I could well find myself playing the perch of a lifetime, but then a surge of water hit me from behind and as I turned and looked at the weir I could see that the lockmaster had just opened one of its gates. Although I continued, this surge of extra water had obviously moved the perch and I saw them go from crawling up my rod, to ghosts.

When it got personal, there was only one outcome.

Filled with mixed emotions I returned to the other side, sat down next to Blobby and poured a coffee while reflecting on my best perch session ever on the weir, but also distraught that another factor, completely out of my control had ruined the day. It was while talking to Blobby about catching a 4lb perch that he mentioned a small day-ticket water called Kingfisher, near to my Bordon home. I looked at him in a bemused manner and said, "If we've got a comfortable water on our doorstep that's got a four-pounder in it, what the bloody hell are we doing here!" The word 'plonker' came to mind, and shortly after, we were on our way home. Blobby was going to show me the venue so that I could return the following day.

Teddington; almost a red-letter day.

Located at Hammer, near Hindhead, Kingfisher was a group of six or more tiny, spring-fed ponds. It had been a trout fishery and although the three ponds above the car park were still fished for trout, the three below had been turned into coarse fisheries. The first thing I remember was the size of these ponds; they were tiny, and an underarm cast was all that was needed to hit the far bank. Set on a hillside, the lakes were well oxygenated from the flowing spring and crystal clear. Small roach dimpled the surface, and with no other anglers in sight I knew that if 4lb perch did exist, then it shouldn't take too long to find them; just how quickly this was to happen was incredible.

I returned the following day, this time with Donut, and vividly remember walking down the frost-covered path to the middle lake that was steaming through the first rays of dawn. I had noticed a swim that had a tree trunk protruding through the water and with a few branches creating some cover and with a small island in front, felt this was obviously a good starting point.

Casting small live baits into position, fished on sunken paternoster rigs, I carefully placed washing-up liquid bottle tops on long drops. It was so much more comfortable than Teddington and far less hassle, and I sat back, relaxed and watched the bobbins swing slowly in the morning breeze.

Five minutes had passed when the left-hand alarm burst into life from a series of irregular bleeps and as I watched the bottle top slowly move upwards, struck into what I expected to be a good perch, yet as it surfaced I was gobsmacked, as it wasn't a perch but a 3lb chub, a species I hadn't been told lived in the lakes.

Donut soon broke his personal best at Kingfisher.

Donut hadn't even cast out and had missed the action as he was visiting the toilet in the car park, so I rested the chub in the landing net. Moments later the other rod burst into life and a stuttery take saw another good fish hooked. I thought that this had to be another chub and gave it some stick, yet when a perch of huge proportions hit the surface I eased off and played the fish with kid gloves. It was then that I realised that I had a chub in the net but luckily, managed to glide the perch over and when I looked down my heart missed a couple of beats.

Donut was by now casually making his way down the footpath and was confronted by me jumping up and down, waving my arms in all directions. He couldn't believe what he saw and once we had regained some

composure, we recorded a weight of 4lb 1oz 8drams for the perch. Pete, the on-site bailiff, arrived and didn't seem that shocked with the catch. He informed us that if we wanted to catch an even bigger perch then we were fishing the wrong lake and needed to investigate the lowest lake which contained a five! As you can imagine, after taking the biggest perch in the middle lake we moved and come the end of the day had taken numerous perch, with Donut recording a 2lb 7oz 8dram best also.

Teddington was forgotten and for the next 18 months these small lakes captivated my mind. This was also the venue where I discovered the effectiveness of prawns for perch; it was Pete who suggested these, and I smile these days when anglers lay claim to having found the new perch wonder-bait, for this was being used by many, more than a decade ago.

The perfect start at Kingfisher.

Although prawns caught fish, they also caught every species in the lake and I have to admit to feeling more comfortable using small livebaits, as anything placed on the bottom of the lake soon saw the hoards of signal crayfish attacking it. Live-baiting was banned, as was spinning, in fact the fishery had so many rules that I'm amazed anyone caught a fish, so in order to be more selective, and catch fish, rules had to be broken.

I fished the bottom lake for the whole of the winter, taking numerous 3lb-plus perch along the way. In fact, 3lb perch became so frequent that I found myself returning any under 3lb 8oz without a photograph! Most sessions saw me arriving well before dawn, sneaking quietly past the bailiff's caravan and managing a few hours before he realised anyone was fishing. I would then pack up mid-morning, head home to complete some work before having lunch, and return for the last couple of hours of light.

Pete, the bailiff, was a strange character and took a percentage of each day ticket in payment for his services, as well as being allowed to live on site. Strange, because I remember him charging me twice in a day, just because I had left the water and returned later; this was something I swallowed for a while and in return, I never thought twice about using lives.

I'm sure he knew and turned a blind eye, as these were used in what I classify as 'stealth mode'; no one was aware that I was using them. I would lip hook a bait, then fold a massive piece of bread flake around it, engulfing the fish, and anyone that happened to be watching thought I was carp fishing. The bread flake normally came off as it hit the surface or floated up after a short sharp pull on the line.

On many of these sessions I would find myself attached to a fish that was to evade capture and started to think that a stray trout had survived and was causing the problem, but looking back I'm sure that on most occasions these were carp that had taken an interest in the red popper used on the paternoster rig and then became foul hooked. However on a couple of occasions, I'm sure what I lost was this massive perch.

Trying to catch this perch became personal, especially after seeing an angler land it on a pole and slip it back without weighing or photographing, as well as hearing it had been caught again, this time on luncheon meat and weighing 5lb 1oz! I knew that I was close to catching this perch and as it was early April knew that this fish would be at its heaviest due to spawning. Plans were made to fish the lake every morning and evening of the week commencing the seventh and it was on the Wednesday morning that week that I finally came face to face with a fish that had filled my mind for so long.

It was a bright, sunny morning and as always I found the small fry dimpling the surface at the bottom end of the lake. Every now and again, a perch would crash through them and as I swung a small roach into position I awaited the inevitable result, but would it be the big one?

A couple of modest perch fell, then, for some reason, I looked to my left and noticed a small clump of lilies that were beginning to sprout, so I cast one of the rods over to them. As I tried to place the bottle top on the line, I found myself struggling, as the bait was intercepted almost immediately and as soon as I struck and hooked the fish I knew which one it was. After a few anxious moments the fish I had spent so much time tracking down was finally mine and looking at the way its belly was rounded with spawn, I knew that I had the fish of a lifetime in front of me.

They say the biggest fish of all is the perch, and when you set eyes on one this size for the first time, it's a statement that's true. Expecting the perch to pull the scales well over the 5lb mark, I remember having to weigh it twice as on both occasions the needle settled just over 4lb 9oz. Slightly confused, I called Blobby and Donut to come down and witness the fish and to bring their scales, as I was doubting mine, but I shouldn't have bothered as my scales were indeed reading correctly.

Typical Kingfisher three-pounder.

After this capture, the eel fishing took up most of my time throughout the summer and although over the moon with my perch, I couldn't help but think whether this fish was the biggest in the lake, so come late August I was back to find out. Numerous threes were caught and with no reports of any perch over four, I began to think the worst, yet come November this was all about to change. England was playing France in the Rugby World Cup and I almost stayed at home but decided to take a small radio and listen to the match while fishing. I can't remember who won because the day was more memorable for a perch, weighing 4lb 4oz, that fell to my livebait tactics.

I continued to fish the lake until March 2004, during which time numerous 3lb perch were caught, some being repeats, and with news of my perch captures leaking out, the lake began to see the odd specialist angler appear.

Finally, in the spring of that year, Simon Scott and Viv Shears gained rights to the water, the day-ticket fishing was lost and they created a carp fish farm throughout.

I know Simon felt quite bad doing this, as he knew it was our secret perch venue, but I think we had seen the best of it by then and he called to say that after netting and draining all the lakes, no 4lb perch were present.

Looking back, I honestly feel that had a bigger perch existed, other than my biggest four, it must have passed away during my time on the water, yet I still think that my perch was the biggest in the lake.

You're not going to catch if you're watching TV!

Crucian carp
Dreams Can Come True

This chapter is based on an article written for Coarse Angling Today. It was originally published in issue 88, December 2008 and everything within it was correct at the time. However, tactics evolve as do the waters fished, so I've brought it up to date.

This account covers a period from the spring of 2003 to the present time, taking me from the ever-in-the-press Harris Lake, on the Marsh Farm complex, to the pinnacle of crucian fishing - you know where - the CEMEX Angling venue in Yateley, and then on to Johnson's Lake run by Godalming Angling Society.

It covers my frustrating, but also rewarding, time on Harris Lake, the capture of two huge crucians from a water I never expected to have the privilege to fish, Little Moulsham, and then to what has to be the best crucian water in the country at the moment, Johnson's. The aim of the article was to inspire, as Ian Welch did to me, any angler who is not scared of going against the grain, has the sheer audacity and cheek to try something completely different, and reap the benefits. If you're up for it then read on. However, if you're happy striking at small dips of a delicate pole float, often foul-hooking and rarely having a red-letter day, then that's fine. I was there once!

Putting down issue 24 of Coarse Angling Today after reading Ian's article, 'Getting Heavy with Crucians' I can only smile and thank him for stirring my imagination. Stumbling on Little Moulsham must have been like winning the lottery for him, and now realising the delicacy of this venue and its position, I have no quarrels with why he kept it secret, allowing just a handful of selected angling friends to participate in such a special place. I was just emerging into the specialist world at the time, and for a couple of years could only watch in awe, as these magical specimens appeared on the pages of the weeklies. I must have

read his article over a dozen times since it was published in August 2003, during which time I have successfully followed in his footsteps, copied his tactics, adjusted them to suit my style of angling and proceeded to catch hundreds of specimen crucians.

Godalming's, Marsh Farm was hitting the headlines at around the same time and 4lb crucians were beginning to feature regularly within catch reports, so without further ado, I decided to take a stroll around the venue and see for myself what all the fuss was about.

At this time, the venue was in its infancy and as can be expected was in complete contrast to that of the Yateley CEMEX Angling water, which I had only found weeks previously and had a sly stroll around. There were no overhanging bushes, lilies, bankside rushes or weed like at Yateley, just a bare, flat landscape housing two islands along with the odd plantation for the future.

Only one angler was on the complex and as I neared him I could see his bright elastic stretching out into the lake. Patiently, I held back, not wanting to intrude, and as he netted the fish I could see that it was a crucian. While he weighed the fish, I entered his swim and as he revealed the crucian from the plastic bag I simply had to pick my jaw up off the ground. Weighing in at 3lb 11oz, it was his second-biggest of the morning. He wasn't able to tell me how many he'd caught as he had lost count and as I sat and watched, he netted two more. He was a regular to the venue and confirmed that catching 20-plus crucians in a morning was commonplace.

The walk to the car became a run, my mind racing as I contemplated when I was able to return. Return I did, but that first summer came and went and after numerous visits to the venue my respectable personal best of 3lb 10oz taken in the summer of 1997 from Frensham Great Pond, accidentally while tench fishing, still stood. The lake became busier by the week, news was spreading quickly throughout the specimen world, but during that first summer I never once saw another angler experience the same ease in which that first angler had caught.

The hype within certain angling weeklies made Marsh look easy, gave the impression that four-pounders were commonplace, and this continued for a number of years. However, now I feel that Harris is far from its best, there are just too many tench, leaving the crucians only one way to go, backwards.

Although thousands were landed, my best was 3lb 13oz.

Dawn breaks across what was once the best crucian water in the country.

I believe that in those early days anglers actually turned up at Marsh for the first time expecting to catch a four straight away; it was hyped up so much. I have to say that not bettering my personal best that first year came as a big disappointment, especially considering the time I'd put in.

Joining the club would bring the benefit of angling through the hours of darkness. Past experience had shown that this was a prime time for catching crucians and it was an edge that I felt any specialist angler needed. Spring is definitely the best time for catching a huge crucian as they increase in weight due to carrying spawn, but don't ignore the autumn, or even early winter, as crucians feed in earnest, gaining reserves that will see them through the colder months.

Unfortunately, with the club ticket running from the 1st of June, all I could do was fish days that spring. By the time the permit came through allowing me to night fish, the crucians had dropped weight due to their energy-sapping activities within the margins, but amazingly, four-pounders were still being reported to the press. Many dedicated specialist anglers joined with the same desire as I did, but very few, if any, succeeded in managing their target and left with a respectable best, a high three.

June the 1st 2004 approached and not forgetting Ian's inspiring piece on bolt rigging for this delicate feeding species, I felt that the hours of darkness would best suit such a diverse tactic. The last thing I wanted was to upset the regular traditionalists, who persisted in using delicate pole floats fished in the margins, with annoying high pitch screams from bite alarms. Another reason for my nocturnal activities was that I knew how effective this type of rig was for other species, and if I could get the balance right, then the crucian would be no exception. Allowing anyone to see its effectiveness, once mastered, just wasn't an option.

Early June saw me descend on Harris Lake, and I remember it well. Swinging my rigs just two-rod lengths out in peg 6, it took no time at all for the alarm to sing and the first of 15 crucians to fall; the best, a memorable brace of 3lb 6oz and 3lb 9oz. The method was far from pretty, but by God it was effective, and I left with the biggest smile imaginable on my face. Numerous overnight sessions accounted for similar results, but from the hundreds of crucians I landed, I never came close to the 4lb barrier. The best was still that 3lb 9oz specimen taken on my first overnight trip.

Marsh was my learning ground and, looking back, my tactics during that first season were far from as effective as they could have been. Fifteen crucians a night seemed a great return but my catch rate would have been so much better if I had used a short, stiff fluorocarbon hooklink instead of the braided one back then. In those early days, 1.5oz fixed leads or small inline feeders were used and although at the time I increased the weight of these too, with the hooking properties of the rig, I now know that changing the hooklink and dropping the size of the hook from a 12 to a 16 would have been better.

The inline method feeders, or leads that carried scalded pellet certainly got the fish into the swim, but overfed, leading to some extremely frustrating nights. Crucian after crucian would roll over the spots, leading to loads of bleeps but resulting in just the occasional take from what should have been a hectic night. I also tried small PVA sticks consisting of a similar mix to Ian's but again, although effective to a point, it became frustrating. I was continuously trying to avoid getting a great big blob of sticky, half-dissolved PVA attached to my hook. PVA may have revolutionised some areas of angling but,

believe it or not, I hardly use it at all. Looking back, scalded pellet should have been avoided and replaced by what I use now, a finely-sieved groundbait.

With the club ticket running to the following June, I was able for the first time, to put my new method into action during the period that saw the crucians at their biggest - February to May. In the cooler months, baits like corn had to be rethought and after a while I settled for double

The groundbait lead accounted for many remarkable catches.

red maggot or caster, which soon brought a personal best of 3lb 11oz. During the period between February and May, it's often the case that every other fish is a three, sometimes more, however after catching literally hundreds of belly-fat fish my best still remained some five ounces short of a four.

Turning the pages of the weeklies revealed more fours and along with a few other dedicated anglers I started to become disillusioned due to these reports. Were we really that unlucky? The penny finally dropped when on two different occasions I was requested to witness crucians of 4lb-plus. This I did, but in doing so I also had to weigh the fish on my scales, digital ones that had been recently tested twice by the weights and measures department due to the capture of two British record fish. Unfortunately, on both occasions the fish weighed a few ounces under the stated weight, much to the disappointment of the angler. Oddly, one of those fish was still reported to the press at his claimed weight. Oh well, that's angling!

Knowing that at the right time of year the venue was capable of supplying a fish of a lifetime, a four-plusser, I continued to visit the lake for the next few seasons, during which time I was able to fine-tune my tactics and land a new personal best of 3lb 13oz.

The most devastating stick-mix at the time was a dry mix of Green Swim-Stim incorporating some hemp and Sonubaits S-Pellets that had just come on to the market. I have never experienced

bubbling like it; the dry groundbait simply explodes out of the PVA in a cloud of stimulants, leaving just the hemp and pellets as feed. This method resulted in many big hauls of crucians, including one of 36 crucians along with numerous tench in an evening. Remarkably, out of all those that evening, just six were over 3lb, the best 3lb 2oz; many of the others were between 2lb 12oz and 2lb 15oz, a familiar return then.

Up-close and personal.

Dad with a big Harris crucian.

Unfortunately, I made the mistake of calling the rig a 'bolt-rig' which was misunderstood by the club as they thought that I was using heavy lines and big hooks, as well as using a fixed weight, which is so far from the truth. My standard set-up, even to this day, consists of a size 16 hook, 4.84lb fluorocarbon hooklink and a 1oz inline lead that is free-running on the main line, certainly not crude, certainly not a 'bolt-rig' and certainly not a method that causes any more mouth damage than other methods.

Little Moulsham - A Breath of Fresh Air.

I couldn't believe my luck. In the shake-up of RMC to CEMEX Angling, Ian had decided to move on to pastures new and as it happened, an old friend, Mick Barnes, had replaced him. Although Ian had invited me to fish Little Moulsham, time restraints had not allowed such a convenient liaison, but my acceptance to produce the occasional article for CEMEX Angling gave me access to the lake that I'd once dreamed of.

My first from Little Moulsham weighed 4lb 1oz.

Was this the last big crucian caught from Moulsham?

Plans were made to fish the lake very early in the spring of 2006. This would mean that I would see the lake wake up from its winter slumber, allowing a better understanding of the lake's moods. Unfortunately, I wasn't alone and it soon became apparent that a couple of other anglers had the same idea. With limited swims available, I rethought my plans and delayed them until mid-June, knowing that these anglers would be moving on to their preferred rivers. Keeping an eye on the lake and what it was producing during the lead-up to the traditional opening of the close season allowed me to put into context just what I was up against.

Between Ian's article and my first legal steps on to the lake, it had been netted, probably early in 2006. Many crucians had been removed, leaving just a few to grow on in the six acres of feature-filled water. I'm still not sure of the numbers but someone said that they thought just two dozen remained. Great! Things were not going to be easy, but I like a challenge.

In the article which had inspired me, Ian had mentioned that he was looking for one run a night, at best, and that was when the head of fish was far greater than it is today. To be honest, I had reasoned on a similar return and even though I was targeting crucians, I was thinking about a run from any species of fish, while I'm sure Ian meant just crucians.

My first experience of angling on the lake was in May, when I arrived to find all the known swims occupied. I slotted into a small gap close by that just allowed a couple of rods to be poked through, and settled back. Nothing positive materialised but I did receive lots of lifts and drops that I now know were crucians. The tench were on a rampage prior to spawning and a greedy red-eye would invariably pick up any bait fished more than a rod length out, or over a good helping of loose feed. One angler however did get on the score sheet with a crucian of exactly 4lb; that was enough for me!

My first session was rather later than I would have liked, however it's not one I will forget as on the 17th of July 2006 I arrived to find the lake empty. That day had been spent at the DEFRA office in Weymouth which saw me arriving late and somewhat unprepared. The rods had been rigged with small method feeders and in my haste to get to the lake I had forgotten the groundbait along with any leads for replacements.

Having pre-baited the swim for over a week I really didn't want to cast these out without any mix around so I made a quick dash to my brother's, grabbing anything that I thought might do. While I was turning the garage upside down, Mick Barnes called asking me to retain any crucian I caught – now, that's being an optimist! It was two hours from the time I'd first arrived at the lake to when I cast in, but as I fixed the bobbin to the slack line on my first cast, the alarm leapt into life, only

momentarily, but enough to alert me to what I thought must be ducks diving.

As I looked out, though, there were no ducks, just an alarm bleeping every now and then. Then the penny finally dropped, not for the first time, and as I picked the rod up a fish was definitely hooked, however it didn't feel of any significance, until it was under the rod and the trademark crucian fight commenced. Crucians aren't the hardest fighting creatures, but when using small hooks and Avon-style rods a headshake can see the hook falling, so it's vital to get things well prepared in such an event. It was then that I realised I had only bought a big, triangular net which was out of position, so trying to manoeuvre this, while playing a fish with kid gloves created a few anxious moments that were really not necessary. Luck was on my side, this time, and a big crucian graced my net; from casting out to getting the bite was literally just seconds!

The call was made and Mick Barnes came down to take the pictures and to witness the fish. His opening words of congratulation cannot be repeated but I took them as a compliment. Carefully, he removed a couple of scales to be sent off for diagnosis to verify this small but thriving, or so I thought, population of crucians, as true crucians.

The following night, I was back with my fine crucian gear and managed to coax a big grass carp into the landing net, only for it to explode in the net and head skyward like an Exocet missile. It was definitely a 30-plus fish and I was gutted at being so close to one of these magnificent creatures yet losing it.

Kevin joined me the next week, and fished a couple of swims on the opposite bank. Unfortunately, he lost a big crucian at first light but his loss was soon forgotten as just as we were packing up he saw a fish swirl, cast to it and soon after was looking at the fish of a lifetime, a grass carp of 36lb 1oz!

The loss of his big crucian had me thinking, so the following week I dropped into the same swim and on two short, overnight sessions I took a personal best crucian of 4lb 3oz 8drams and a personal best grass carp of 32lb 2oz. As much as I wanted to run around the lake naked in my routine personal best salute, I declined the thought because there were too many brambles, nettles, and mosquitoes, so I just breathed in the atmosphere and enjoyed the moment. That week I also landed a bream, the only one I have ever heard of coming from the lake.

For some reason, I decided to leave the lake alone, probably due to the autumn approaching, but it was a decision that I was to regret come the following season. Other species were calling and I knew that what I had learned over such a short period on the lake would be put into great effect the following spring. Then a publication asked if I could investigate the potential of Harris once more. It was late August, a time when crucians should be at their lowest weight but an influx of reported four-pounders made me sceptical.

I chose a hot, humid day and arrived to find little being caught. Positioning myself away from the crowds, I swung my now tried and tested rigs into position.

Come first light, 58 crucians had fallen to the aforementioned tactics, including 19 threes, to a best of 3lb 5oz. All the fish were lean and completely empty. August isn't a month when you see crucians at their heaviest, far from it; they are probably at their lowest weight. If a lake is producing fours throughout the summer, then back in the spring we would have seen these same fish pushing the British record, so why weren't we seeing this? I think my statistics speak for themselves. However, as I said earlier, believe what you want to believe; that's angling. Just a thought, maybe I should get my scales checked again, maybe they're weighing 12oz light!

Although I still occasionally visit Harris Lake, it's either to complete a magazine feature or to show another angler this devastating rig. Harris Lake is still a fantastic venue and multiple catches of specimen crucians are still possible, but it has to be classified now as a mixed fishery and not the specimen venue for which it was once famous.

The spring of 2007 couldn't come quickly enough and I remember walking across the football pitch, straining my neck to get my first glimpse of Little Moulsham. It's a really gorgeous lake with mature trees and bushes creating a canopy of cover around its gin-clear margins. The smell of wild watermint crushed underfoot creates a heady aroma and every time I descend on its bank, I'm taken back years to my childhood days, probably because of its intimate quiet nature, something that's difficult to find nowadays. Thoughts of a sustained campaign, along with numerous massive crucians gracing my net filled my imagination, but little did I know at the time that a stocking of carp earlier in the year was going to make crucian fishing almost impossible. The lake was also losing some of its natural beauty as the following season it was to become a CEMEX Angling syndicate venue, and pathways, new swims and fencing started to show. However, what interested me more lived subsurface.

I remember falling asleep listening to the distant church bells and recall counting 12, a time that saw one of my alarms burst into what I thought was crucian mode. The fight was unspectacular and whatever was on the other end had me fooled right until my head torch illuminated it; yes, it was that bloody bream again!

The double swim that had become famous at Little Moulsham for its huge crucians fell silent and from getting a bite on a good night, I was lucky to get a liner. I started to move around the lake, carefully baiting spots in the margins before placing my baits on top, but it seemed that crucian life had ended.

Opportunist fishing at its best.

Drastic action saw baits fished further out, yet the only action was from the stockie carp that instantly smashed up my fragile rigs. Before long, I was landing these, yet remember thinking that I was no longer crucian fishing, but carp fishing, and with no reports of crucian captures or sightings I assumed that either the small population had come to the end of their days, or that numbers were so small that targeting them was just not viable.

I still walk around the lake on the odd occasion, looking through Polaroids under the bushes in the margins, but all I see are massive grass carp and the occasional tench. It was on one such circuit that I bumped into Tony Gibson who was also targeting the crucians. He was faring in the same way and knowing how dedicated and talented this angler is, I thought, 'if he can't catch them, what chance have I?' I'm sure that one day we will see a truly massive crucian once again coming from the lake, but for me my time had come, it was time to say goodbye.

Although the thought of catching a crucian carp bigger than my personal best still fills my mind, in reality the chance of doing this seems to be slipping away. Harris

Kevin's results were mind-blowing.

Lake as well as Little Moulsham had peaked earlier in my angling career and having spent so much time searching on these waters, I started to feel that the possibility of achieving such a goal was history. Obviously, there are massive crucians still to be caught but many will be accidental captures and for the specialist angler wanting to target them, venues are slowly disappearing.

Godalming Angling Society's Johnson's Lake, or as I used to know it, Enton, has had a history for years of containing massive crucians and it was from here that Harris got its stocking. I joined Godalming Angling Society in 2009, but I was unsuccessful that year in unlocking Johnson's true potential. However, in the summer of 2011, a couple of very big fish recaptured my interest.

Kevin had also joined and it was a catch early on in the season that showed the venue's true potential, as one afternoon he pole-fished off the dam to take numerous crucians to well over 3lb. My first visit also saw numerous crucians caught; this time I used a 15-foot rod, centrepin and a delicate pole float to present a soft pellet and take crucians to 3lb 9oz.

Johnson's is now the place to be.

Massive brace taken in October.

Thinking we had found heaven, we returned only to be brought back to earth, as further visits throughout the summer saw us struggling. More often than not, just buying a positive bite during the day was a result, yet as darkness fell the odd crucian would make a mistake, but it was the size of some of the crucians that rolled in front of us that kept drawing us back, especially Kevin and Dad.

As the summer disappeared and autumn arrived, Kevin's results started to pick up. Come September, he had fine-tuned his approach and with the fish feeding hard before winter arrived, he started to make some historic catches. Some evenings, he was losing count of the crucians over 3lb and many weren't just scraper threes but big threes, and the more he fished the bigger they got.

I was gagging to join him but with a diary booked with guiding days, features and weddings, I had just to sit back and watch as he crept ever closer to the magical 4lb barrier, then one evening, the phone rang requesting my photography skills as he had just taken a brace weighing 3lb 15oz and 3lb 14oz!

Luckily, come October I was able to start meeting up with him and cash in on the action. We tried to keep the feed going into the swims every other night, a tactic that seemed to work, as on every session we recorded multiple catches of 3lb crucians and most were now over 3lb 8oz. Kevin really had the bit between his teeth, fishing far more frequently than I was, and once again, I found myself taking a call, late one evening, requesting my assistance. This time, though, he had broken the magical 4lb barrier with a crucian of 4lb 3oz and while I was on my way, he had landed another specimen of 3lb 15oz.

In late October, after catching lots of threes, I managed to break the four; with one of 4lb 1oz. The action continued, probably down to the mild winter, and come mid-November we were still catching on most nights, yet the action was tailing off considerably and later that month, we finally called it a day.

An after-dark four-pounder from Johnson's in October.

Pumpkinseed British record

Sway Lake New Forest

Sway Lakes in the New Forest has always been known for its shoals of very big roach and it was these that I had the intention of catching. Previous trips had proved fruitless and although the lake was perfect for fishing the waggler, a method I'm at complete ease with, for one reason or another it just didn't happen for me.

The scales never lie.

It might be small, but it's a record.

The fish were spawning, the weather was just too bright, or the fish were at the opposite end of the lake to where I was fishing. As we all progress through our angling life, some waters are kind, others aren't, and Sway was a venue that just didn't like me.

It was a boiling hot day, sending every roach heading for the cover of the far bank reeds or lily pads. Feeding was the last thing on their minds and although a few roach were landed, the best fell well short of the targeted two-pound barrier and It was other species that kept us busy. Just after landing a good perch, I momentarily dropped my hookbait in the margins then, on lifting, realised that I had hooked something.

I swung it to hand and was dumbfounded as I had absolutely no idea what the fish was. It looked like a brightly-coloured piranha. Donut had joined me and soon identified it as a sun bass, a species similar to one that he had seen in France. He also mentioned that they are usually much smaller than the 3oz specimen I was holding, and was soon on the phone to the news desk at Anglers Mail. They also seemed somewhat perplexed and after an hour or so returned the call, identifying the fish as a pumpkinseed and said that the record stood at 4oz 9drams.

During this time, I had set up a small pole float and had been catching numerous pumpkinseeds, the biggest going 5oz 8drams, so you can imagine our surprise when we heard the news. Furthermore, I had been dropping these into my landing net in the margins.

Blobby had also joined us, so having two independent witnesses, photographs were taken and the fish re-weighed on a couple of sets of scales before I drank in the atmosphere and felt the excitement of having just broken a record that had stood for many years. Back at home, the necessary paperwork was sent over and a record claim submitted to the BRFC. The procedure was long-winded as the fish had to be identified and scales checked.

It appeared in Anglers Mail the following week and its capture created a cult following for the species, with anglers claiming that they knew of venues that held far bigger specimens. Tanyards Fishery in West Sussex was one such venue and it was Bill Rushmere who increased the record further with the capture of an incredible specimen weighing an astonishing 14oz, which still stands to this day. I did return to Sway, once again with roach on my mind, but as before, they did a disappearing act on the day and I had to be content catching numerous quality perch as well as a few pumpkinseeds, which included a personal best of 11oz.

Finally, my certificate came, almost a year since the capture. However, at the bottom, the words 'Interim Coarse Fish Record' were somewhat of a disappointment, and to this day I proudly display this certificate in my lavatory!

I didn't have a clue what I had caught.

Old Father Thames - carp

River Thames

From a very early age, I have had a passion for the River Thames and recall days spent casting feeders up against the moored boats on Fry's Island, where we caught quality roach and pike that were intent on robbing us of our silver adversary.

During my match days, Kevin and I would practise our pole fishing skills along the promenade at Caversham, where in the right conditions we would catch good nets of perch, roach and dace, by holding back hard just off the edge of the cabbages.

Knowing that bream were in the area, we soon progressed once winter arrived, finally locating these around the island downstream of Scours Lane at Tilehurst. Casting maggot feeders tight against the island and using long hooklinks, sometimes upwards of six feet, we would pay out plenty of line and watch the quiver-tip for the slightest of taps. Tiny taps were all we received, never the steady and confident pull round we have now come to expect, but they were big bream and with the odd chub thrown in, these were happy days and ones I remember so vividly.

On the odd occasion a fish would be hooked that had one thing on its mind, the sanctuary of the island snags, and it shattered our frail tackle. These were probably carp or barbel but we never found out as none of us ever landed one. As they say 'you can get too much of a good thing' and as the prime swims were becoming increasingly popular, and the match scene moved to carp puddles, we moved too, completely away from the competitive world, finally settling on a venue some would call my second home, Frensham Great Pond. It was a venue I simply fell in love with and the Thames was forgotten. Would I ever return?

Sea fishing was also something my father taught me from a very young age and although I looked forward to these trips, usually ended up feeling seasick, swallowing a couple of Kwells and then lying in the boat wishing I was back on land. I remember one outing so well; it was in the very early days and at the time we had a Norwegian-built 12ft clinker Rana boat that we launched from the HMS Daedalus slipway at Lee-on-Solent. Looking back, how four of us managed to get in this boat still amazes me, yet as I said, my brother Kevin and I were still very young. A petrol Seagull engine motored us slowly west to The Brambles, well across to the Isle of Wight, and I recall anchoring up next to a red buoy on the edge of the shipping lane. There we caught plenty of smoothhounds, thornback rays, dogfish and pouting and once the tide turned, making fishing impossible, we headed back to shore.

Halfway back, and while lying in the boat once more feeling like death, I looked skywards and felt that we were going around in circles. Circles were exactly what we were doing and as the four of us peered over the side looking at the motor, all that was seen was the propeller falling off and sinking out of sight. The smell of petrol filled the air, making me feel even worse, and I recall Dad and Wally having to row what seemed many miles back to shore. That was the end of the clinker-built boat yet Dad was still enthusiastic and decided to buy a CJR 14-foot cruiser, along with a Marina 30hp motor, and a new propeller for the Seagull engine that was stored as a back-up.

Our trips continued, but not without incident. I recall a day when we headed for the Nab Tower, around 11 miles offshore, yet halfway there we decided this was a bit adventurous and settled on a mark somewhere en route. It was a fantastic day, calm and clear, and the ever-obliging dogfish kept us interested. We didn't notice a thick fog gradually descending, one that completely engulfed us and having just a small, hand-held compass, we headed slowly back to shore with me constantly blowing the boat's horn. I say 'slowly' because here we were in the middle of a busy shipping lane, completely blind, as were all the other boats that were around us at that time. It was a nerve-racking experience, one that really bought home the dangers of being afloat in such a tiny craft, knowing that a cross-Channel ferry could have hit and crushed us. We finally made it to shore, albeit miles to the east of Langstone Harbour, and from that day we fished within sight of

land, often in the harbours, float fishing for flounder or bass. The sea fishing continued for a couple of years but it was never really something I enjoyed, even after overcoming the seasickness, and eventually the boat was placed in storage at my uncle's home.

Some years after, my uncle sadly passed away and his property was sold so the boat had to find a new home and for a while it sat in the front garden at my house in Bordon, without moving. Dad had checked the motor, but even after serious greasing before it went into storage and the years of redundancy, the salt water had done the damage and it was scrapped for spares.

Launching the bait boat at Caversham.

If it weren't for this fish, we would have given up.

It was also a time when I was fishing Teddington Weir, perch were making the headlines, and it was these that were my target. However, unlike every other spot on the Thames, it wasn't a place I warmed to even after catching my fair share of perch to over 3lb.

I was looking for something new in my world of angling and the appearance of two very big carp in the press, caught from the Thames, and having a boat at my disposal, set my mind working and after discussing this opportunity with my father we decided to split the cost and equip the boat for a new adventure.

First on the list was obviously a motor. A powerful motor wasn't needed because the Thames has a speed limit of approximately five miles an hour, so after a bit of research we opted for a 15hp Suzuki. The next step was to insure the boat, as well as buying the annual registration plate needed, which is based on the length of the boat and allows you to navigate through the locks. Also needed was a Boat Safety Scheme Certificate, it's a bit like a car's MOT, lasts for three years and costs around £80. All in all, the cost spiralled far beyond what we initially expected, but we had come too far and by now there was no turning back. We both knew that we had to catch some mighty fish to justify such a pricey outlay.

This organising took a few weeks and sadly, the start of the season passed, the eel fishing on the Heath was as good as ever, and it wasn't until mid-July that we took our first tentative steps into a whole new adventure. Towing for the first time was scary and with the boat so light it was easy to forget it was behind you, only for it to start swinging dangerously once the speedometer exceeded 50mph.

The first couple of outings were without rods as we wanted to practise launching the boat and steering it through the locks, both easier said than done as the boat sits high on the water and having very little hull, swings from side to side very easily, and as for the public slipway at Caversham, it can only be described as a joke.

The main reason is that the slipway doesn't gradually slide away to the bottom of the river, but stops suddenly, leaving a couple of feet drop. That's not a problem in the winter when the river is high, but during a warm summer and low water levels, to get the boat to slide easily off the trailer meant having to rest the trailer tyres just inches from this drop-off.

Launching was far easier than extracting the boat from the river at the end of the session and the thought of this really took the pleasure out of what should have been a relaxing day. Added to this danger was the local bakery, which irresponsibly decided to feed their leftovers to the thousands of swans that live on the river, and they do this right on the slipway. This brings a whole new meaning to the word 'slipway' and I found myself cursing and attending to the cuts and bruises caused by slipping over on the huge amount of swan poo.

On one occasion, we secured the boat with a rope and used it as a winch around the tow bar to lower the boat slowly down the slipway, which worked a treat until someone decided to park right across its entrance, something that we found happened more often than not.

The last straw came when we had been out on the river all day, only to find the entrance blocked, once again. We managed to get the trailer down the side of this car and on to the slipway, attach a rope then extend this up over the bonnet of the parked car around the towing hitch and with Dad pushing and me pulling we made some sort of headway in retrieving the boat. To be honest, I gave little thought to the rope that had to be causing some paint damage to the parked car, but the problems really started when I slipped, probably on swan poo, which saw the boat upending, leaving the motor on the ground and the front of the boat and trailer up in the air. There were some choice words exchanged between my father and I, although these should have been aimed at the owner of the parked car. Fortunately, and somewhat embarrassingly, the local canoe club had been watching with amusement and I had to go and ask for their assistance in salvaging the situation.

Those initial trips from 'swan poo slipway' weren't wasted, as they gave us plenty of practice through the locks, and where we were once entering the lock in slalom fashion we were now silky smooth. Well not quite!

The days spent on the river around Caversham had revealed just one sighting of a carp, a common so big that it took my breath away, and just a week after that sighting I found myself looking at what could have been the same fish, a 30 caught by Chris Berry. This fish was spotted just downstream of Scours Island and my thoughts reflected back to those bream fishing days. Was this one of the unseen monsters that had smashed us up many years before? Probably!

Above Maple Durham Lock there was an altogether different stretch and the amount of carp we spotted far outweighed that of the area around Caversham. It was also idyllic with the sloping hills of the Chilterns creating a fantastic backdrop, and it was here that we obviously decided to settle. The problem here was although the stretch held a number of carp, none

What a brace! Taken in daylight at the same time.

A stunning, fully-scaled mirror.

looked the size of the common at Caversham, yet we needed confidence and size wasn't a consideration, we just needed a capture.

The stretch also has only a few areas of free fishing. Reading and District AA have a wooded stretch near Maple Durham House and looking at their website, the odd carp was shown but what also figured in captures were barbel. The opposite bank to this is featureless but fishing is allowed and after what would be a long walk from Maple Durham Lock, a small island is found and it was here that we came across a carp angler who was bivvied up. This was a very rare sight and in all the days of fishing through this area and the Pangbourne stretch, I can honestly say that I could count the carp anglers on one hand; looking back, it was probably the same angler.

Above the island and opposite Hardwick House, there are 'no mooring' and 'no fishing' signs which extend right up to the National Trust field below the toll bridge next to Whitchurch Lock, which is an area of free, overnight mooring. It's also a free fishing zone and the far bank is full of features albeit shallow and silty.

Above the R&DAA section and right up to in front of Hardwick House it is once again signed as a no mooring and no fishing area, which is a shame as this middle section was where most of the carp were spotted sunning themselves between the cabbages.

There is a fallen tree above the island on the Hardwick House bank and every time we passed it we saw carp, maybe as many as 20, yet although we discussed mooring where we weren't meant to be, and fishing for them, we never did. Trying to appear inconspicuous in an orange boat isn't easy!

Above the house was a field that was obviously fished, and an area where we spotted carp, but we would have to wait until the following summer before we found out details of the fishing rights so we finally settled in a £5 a night mooring spot on the bank at Bozedown Alpaca Farm. Although this field had 'no fishing' signs along its bank, the signs were old, worn and almost unreadable and when the workers from the farm came down to collect the money from us they said that fishing was allowed for boat mooring, they were just there to stop anglers taking the spaces which would see them lose out on mooring fees.

A wood carving if ever there was one.

At one point we couldn't go wrong, wherever we settled.

As you can imagine, the swims were wide and comfortable as they had been created with narrowboats in mind, the only drawback was that either side of the swims saw loads of fallen trees, snags that would take no prisoners. We fished these swims on numerous occasions during the day, leaving the car and trailer in the public car park at Caversham, something I never felt very comfortable with and as the summer progressed we decided to leave this overnight, fish the night, and then head back as soon as the locks opened the following morning. We also saw a slipway at the boatyard at the bottom of Scours Lane, something that would be our saviour the following year.

I'm not sure how many day sessions we fished, but what we did know was that we weren't far away from carp and that day sessions, although producing the odd bream and chub, were probably not the best for carp. We needed to do a night and it was a decision that was to see our fortune change.

You can't mistake a proper Thames carp.

Here are the words taken from my diary of that session

River Thames, Tuesday 5th August 2003.

What follows can only be described as a mini adventure, one that will never be forgotten. Left home at midday on Tuesday for a 24-hour session somewhere deep in the Berkshire countryside. Launched the boat at Caversham and headed upstream towards Oxford, through the first lock to a stretch where we have always spotted carp. Around 20 were spotted sunning themselves opposite the canoe club, an inaccessible area, but we settled some 200 yards upstream in the hope of attracting them upstream to our baited area.

Placing 60 balls of particle feed on the far bank, plus the same on an inside line, we settled back, hoping for carp. Soon the swim was alive with fish but these turned out to be bream and during the night 13 were landed, including a personal best of 7lb 7oz for Dad.

Two chub put in an appearance, the largest 3lb 8oz, both on corn, in-close. The highlight of the session, though, came at 12.10am when Dad hooked and landed a mirror carp weighing 17lb11oz, another personal best. Things could have been even better but I lost two carp, one that felt very big, from hook pulls, but that's fishing. At last we are off the mark and things feel so much better.

Looking back, I can't remember losing those two fish, yet I can remember shaking Dad's hand, celebrating his capture and knowing that we had almost ironed everything else out, ready for an onslaught, but due to a two-week holiday, the summer slipped away and we only fished the Thames again twice more that season. Those sessions both produced numerous bream, in fact loads of bream and we were forced to switch from single 14mm boilies to snowman rigs consisting of much larger baits.

The first of these two trips was the last time we used the slipway at Caversham, as while buying something for the boat, in the boatyard at Tilehurst, we asked about the possibility of using their private slipway. Not only was the answer favourable but they also agreed that we could leave our car and trailer in the back of the boatyard, which was locked, for just a fiver a day. It was music to our ears and the only drawback was that the slipway could only be used during trading hours, a problem that was easily solved as the following year we decided to fish two night sessions. The last piece of the jigsaw had been placed; all we could do was wait for the arrival of June the 16th the following year, when we would return to settle the score.

Although a door had momentarily closed, another opened and the privilege to fish a private stretch of the river Itchen created a welcome distraction over the winter.

When the new season opened the following year, we were both eager to return and we tried to fish the Thames at least once a week. It was during one of our trips up the Thames that we once again saw the carp angler, this time fishing the island above Maple Durham Lock. We stopped for a chat and made ourselves out as everything but carp anglers. The flood gates then opened, even to the extent of this angler taking out a photo album with images of numerous carp captures from the Thames. I remember noticing that there were no monsters included, the best was probably a low-20, but he commented on a ghostie common that was the jewel in that stretch's crown, one he was eager to catch.

First light was often a feeding period, as Dad found out.

Part of the Thames adventure.

Unfortunately, it wasn't until the second week of July that I caught my first Thames carp and this came from a new swim opposite a small stream that entered the river, once again in the alpaca field. We settled down in this swim, as our normal position had a wasp nest in it, deposited the usual bombardment of Vitalin and watched as the bream arrived and the liners started.

As darkness fell, a very good fish rolled over the baited area and both Dad and I were sure that it was a carp. Bream after bream came to the net before things quietened down around midnight. This was the standard behaviour and our thoughts were that the bream would sense the bait straight away, head upstream and devour most of it. Once they had eaten, they would move out of the swim, yet the disturbance from them ripping the bottom up and colouring the water would, in turn, attract the carp that were inquisitive and came to investigate. The small items, like hemp that were left got them searching and Yateley Angling's Squirrel Snowman hook baits were like cherries on a cake.

It was 1am when the indicator tightened and vibrated against the rod blank. By now I had learned the art of fishing locked-up, and knew that a bream would only cause a massive dropback, so I was out of the sleeping bag in a flash. This fish would be kiting on a tight line downstream and if not stopped, would just head into the near bank snags. Bending into the fish, I started to pump it as quickly as possible, gaining line in the hope that when it surfaced, it would be under my feet but it wasn't to be and just downstream everything went solid.

I have to admit that I felt like crying at that moment as I knew I was so close, only to be tricked at the last obstacle. Dad was crouching by my side, ready with the net and realised how disappointed I was. All I could do was slacken off and hope the carp would swim out, but after what seemed hours all I could do was point the rod at the snag and pull for a break. It was then that something started to move, and as our head torches shone into the crystal clear water a huge branch came into view and below it was a carp.

Dad struggled to net the fish but eventually she went in and at long last and after all the hard work, I'd finally got what I'd come for, A Thames carp. On the scales she went 19lb 12oz and was a fish I will never forget. It seemed that this was the opening of the flood gates, as from that moment on, we hardly lost another fish. In fact, in the early hours I found myself attached to another carp, this time weighing 14lb 15oz.

Three more sessions passed and all produced a carp, but nothing massive; the best weighed 16lb 1oz. It was early August and after a torrential downpour we had a red-letter session, although it was disaster for the tidal Thames because the sewers, unable to take the volume of water, poured raw sewage into the river, which removed the oxygen and killed everything in its path.

These are the words taken from my dairy:
River Thames, 2nd to 4th August 2004.

A red-letter day that makes up for what's been an uneventful season so far. The two-hours travelling saw us arrive at our chosen swim at around 2pm. As we set up, a carp crashed, so expectations were high. Baited with 15 kilos of tiger nuts, maples, trout pellet, corn and boilies laced in Vitalin, plus a sloppy trout pellet mixture that was used as a scent leak-off which soon had bream activity in our swim.

Eight or more bream came to our net early on, but we had to wait until 4am before the first carp was landed; a fully-scaled mirror of 23lb 10oz. At 11am I lost a carp on Dad's rods, which took me completely by surprise while Dad was taking a leak.

Little happened until the afternoon and after Mother called, warning us of a powerful storm, we found ourselves holding down the ovals for dear life. The storm passed and what followed was amazing, as not one, but numerous carp showed themselves in a way that was more like salmon scaling a waterfall!

Shortly afterwards, between 5pm and 7pm, Dad received three runs, landing carp of 11lb 6oz and 17lb 6oz plus, unfortunately, losing one due to boat traffic. Changing my tiger nut rod over to squirrel boilie and re-casting saw both rods fly off together around 8pm resulting in the much sought-after ghostie common of 21lb 8oz and Dad taking the other rod which resulted in a mirror of 22lb 5oz.

The decision not to introduce any more bait was made and we were thinking we had made a wrong move but at 2am and 4am my rods screamed off, resulting in a mirror of 20lb 2oz and a fully-scaled mirror of 15lb 10oz. What a session, and one I will never forget.

Dusk over the Chilterns.

Apart from a small chub to Dad's rod, no more action came. The swim was filled in with Vitalin as we left at 9am anticipating our next assault. When we arrived home, the sad news filtered through of the situation on the tidal. Although excited from our session, the moment was somewhat saddened by this tragedy.

The swim continued to produce, but our paradise was to be cut short as while on an intended two-day stint in early September, and after the capture of a stunning 22lb 10oz fully-scaled mirror on the first morning, an angler arrived and informed us that the stretch was in fact run by a syndicate and that we would have to leave. The reason for not seeing another angler during the summer months was explained, that due to boat mooring the members don't normally start fishing until the autumn. I did ask for information regarding the syndicate but he refused to pass this over, so as he turned his back I lifted the sack that contained the carp, smiled at him and thought that it was probably a good time to move on anyway.

It was our last visit to the Thames that season but our time afloat had revealed many other spots throughout

This has to be the best-looking carp I have ever caught.

the stretch, as well as upstream of Whitchurch Lock and knowing that we'd had our fill on the stretch below, we looked forward to a new challenge the following year.

Our partnership continued throughout the winter, mostly on the river Loddon. It was a time when I was trying to beat my barbel best that stood at 10lb 15oz and little did I know that Carter's Hill would produce a river record to my rod, one weighing 16lb 10oz, a personal best that still stands to this day.

The following season (2005), we were back much earlier and our eyes were opened as wherever we settled along the Thames, carp graced our nets. The first area was the Child Beale stretch, an area the carp angler had told us about, but we didn't fish the island swims that not only needed pruning, but also showed signs of other anglers fishing long sessions - need I say more? Instead, we headed for the comfort of the opposite bank.

That first session saw Dad land a mirror of exactly 15lb, as well as miss a screamer. The National Trust park below Whitchurch Lock was our next settling point and after a recast at dawn to a carp that crashed downstream, my rod roared off and a stunner weighing 16lb 3oz dropped into the net. The Island Swim downstream also produced, and over a two-night session we landed carp of 15lb 1oz, 16lb 15oz and a common of 21lb 1oz.

Although I wanted to fish the Thames as much as I could, other venues were taking up my time. Marsh Farm and its huge crucians was one of these, as was Mill Farm Fishery, which was too deliver my second British record. I also got an invitation to fish CEMEX Angling's Westhampnett; little did I know then, what an important part this venue would play in later years.

So it wasn't until late July that Dad and I found ourselves afloat again, leisurely heading upstream to a big snag swim we'd found during earlier sessions. As we passed Hardwick House we noticed a gentleman fishing a cane rod and wearing a flat cap. It really was a scene from the Mr Crabtree years and we decided to investigate because this was an area where many a carp had been spotted. The gentleman was full of information and passed on details of the syndicate, which we duly joined. We didn't fish it that year as upstream, the snag was just about to reveal its true potential.

The Snag swim was a free overnight mooring section, popular throughout the summer, so we had to arrive early afternoon to get a position opposite the feature, because later in the afternoon, and once the locks had stopped being operated, fleets of boats would head for this area. This was our fourth new spot of the year and until now we hadn't failed to catch a carp, and sure enough, in the early hours, a 16lb 8oz mirror graced my net.

The following week, we couldn't get a position along this stretch due to a regatta taking place so we decided on the National Trust park once more, yet although bream and chub kept us interested, it was to be our first carp blank in ages.

The next trip to the snag swim produced two carp, with Dad taking an 18lb 7oz mirror, a new personal best, but the summer had passed, and as autumn arrived, launching the boat became problematic. The nights were drawing in and becoming damp, cold and long, so with Dad preferring to stay at home, I headed to the Thames on my own, finally finding my way to the snag swim after a long walk on foot.

My first session on my own was one to remember because I landed three carp. The first came at midnight, a time that many a carp was caught. After sacking her up, I recast and drifted off only to be awoken at 3am by another carp of 18lb 4oz. I had only taken one sack, so decided to take a quick picture of the first carp and sack the bigger one until morning. This was when I realised that my camera battery was flat and, unable to take a picture, I released the smaller of the two back into the river. I struggled to sleep after that, as I wanted a picture of every carp I caught from the Thames and just laid there trying to figure out what to do.

As darkness gave way to light, my left-hand rod screamed into life and after a nerve-racking, powerful fight, I slid the net under yet another carp, this time even bigger than the one resting in the sack. On the scales she weighed 23lb 13oz, one of my biggest so far from a campaign that was now into its third summer and I felt gutted as I slid an 18-pounder back into the Thames without a picture.

With the 20 safely sacked, I remembered someone saying that warming a battery might just inject some life into it, so as I lay in my sleeping bag I held the battery tightly in my hand and under my armpit. Two hours passed and I slid the battery back into the camera and couldn't believe that it showed signs of life, but just how much? I managed to organise everything, set the focus on the fish and lift her while the timer light flashed. 'Please, please don't stop', I remember saying to myself. The shutter clicked and a further three images were taken before the battery life ended, but it was enough, and I headed for the car just hoping that the pictures would be useable.

That weekend I was the photographer at a wedding at Frensham Pond Hotel and as I parked up in the car park, I noticed an air-drying sack full of boilies hanging from a post in the car park. It was around 10am and I expected the angler who had placed them there to collect them later that day, and was surprised to find them still there when I left the hotel close to midnight, so I placed the bag in the car and thought, 'I will use these on Monday night in the Snag swim'. Whoever made these boilies did a great job as they accounted for four carp that night.

Here are the words taken from my diary of this session: **River Thames, 29th September 2005.**

It just keeps getting better. Arrived by boat at 5pm, weather's fine and mild but coming in wet at 2am before drying up at dawn. The weatherman has got it almost right as the rain started at 9pm not 2am. Squirrel bottom baits on one and a boilie wrapped in paste on the other, but just as the confidence was going on Squirrel, it produces the goods. 7pm, 19lb 1oz odd-shaped mirror with deformed gill covers, 1.30am, 21lb 3oz mirror, 5am, 18lb 13oz and 6am, 12lb 5oz mirror.

Dad sat next to me for just a couple of bream and I must admit at feeling somewhat guilty, but that's fishing. Squirrel boilies wrapped in a good helping of paste worked better than just the boilie, accounting for three of my four carp. I feel that the baits are getting masked with dying weed after a few hours and need to be re-cast every four hours or so. I've also learned to use back-leads directly under the rods as this stops a hooked fish wiping the other rods out. 12lb 5oz, 18lb 13oz, 19lb 1oz and another 20, this time 21lb 13oz. What a night!

With the carp fishing on the Thames being so good, I could have easily cancelled the two-week holiday that followed, but it was a trip to the Ebro at Capse with Martin Walker of Catfish Capers, yet my aim was to see my dad hook and land a catfish in excess of 100lb. The holiday certainly lived up to expectations.

It was late October 2005 when I returned to the Snag swim and although I did catch a carp weighing 16lb 11oz, it was to be the last, and further visits drew blanks. Whether these carp moved away to deeper, warmer water or just stopped feeding I'm not sure, but the lack of action and the cold nights were draining my confidence and I finally decided enough was enough come early December.

The barbel at Carters were in an obliging mood throughout the winter and although the Thames trips were too demanding for Dad, he did join me on the odd occasion at Carters and during one session landed two massive fish weighing 12lb 5oz and 13lb 12oz, bigger than any brace I've ever caught. We also continued to enjoy the grayling and roach fishing on the Itchen that winter.

Although caught twice, Dad only accepted this as a personal best once.

I never expected anything like this.

The spring bought another invitation to fish Westhampnett and my personal best carp was caught weighing 31lb 13oz, yet it was the Thames that was on the verge of producing a fish of a lifetime.

The start of the 2006 river season arrived and tropical conditions gripped the country. The river was in a poor state with hardly any flow and the locks were time-consuming to navigate because the lock keeper had been instructed to save water and was only allowing movement through when these were full of boats. The tops of the weirs even had sandbags placed along

them to retain the water and the first couple of trips to the Snag swim failed to produce.

We also saw the odd dead carp that had obviously failed to recover from an early spawn. Couple this with a wheel-bearing on the trailer collapsing en route to the river, our plans over the next few weeks were abandoned and it wasn't until August 2007 that we returned. Our return was without the boat, as we had decided to try the new syndicate stretch which was easily accessible and an easy walk to the swims.

The new stretch immediately showed that it had potential and that first night I landed two carp weighing 20lb 9oz and 14lb 4oz, but it could have been better, as in the earlier hours two bream hung themselves on my rigs. All I can remember was the odd bleep on the rods. It was a problem that was to haunt me on my second trip as after taking a carp of 13lb 15oz, I watched as the rod tip knocked but the alarm failed to register. These bream were small, around two pounds, and although the set-up was exactly as I had used for years, it needed to be altered and its sensitivity either increased, or changed to a set-up that would deter the bream.

It was a time when the chod rig was all the rage, so on the next visit I was armed with bright pop-ups and instead of the Vitalin came a big bucket of hemp and tigers. As I spodded these out, it soon became apparent that the new approach had worked as no bream were spotted over the baited area, but would the carp find the bait? The answer came a few hours later as after a bleep on one of the rods, I watched as the indicator pulled tight and vibrated. Bending into the fish, I knew straightaway that what had picked up my bait was something special, but with a nasty snag downstream, simply gave the fish as much stick as I dared before Dad slid the net under what I would consider to be the best-looking carp I have ever caught. It was also my biggest from the Thames and weighed 26lb 13oz. However, little did I know that just two weeks later I would be holding something far bigger.

I was back at the Snag swim, and with an injection of rain the river looked and felt far more appealing, although the previous two sessions had only produced bream. Dad had once again joined me and we had arrived by boat. Loads of pellet and boilies were dropped next to the feature and we sat back awaiting events to unfold. The bream were spotted upstream and were working their way downstream but luckily, they stopped 50 yards or so above the snag and didn't bother us that night.

At 2am I hooked my first carp which weighed 19lb 14oz and settled back, contented. Dad's always awake at daybreak and I had put the kettle on for the much awaited brew that tastes so good at that time, when a bleep on my rods had me watching. As I'd come to expect, the indicator tightened and vibrated and as I watched the rod tip lower, and the back lead move, I knew that a carp was hooked.

The fish headed slowly downstream, away from the snag and started to kite towards the near bank and with just a few cabbages to contend with I felt in total control, that was until a massive common hit the surface and in a great big splash, sped across the river with the clutch screaming. Never had I hooked a carp so powerful on the Thames and I knew that this fish was special in every sense of the word. In the net she finally went and after punching the air and shouting aloud, we lifted her on to the mat. This fish was a stunner and as I watched the dial move past 20, and then 30, I knew that a dream had come true. At 31lb 15oz Id just caught a personal best that lives on today.

That was our last carp that year and although the Thames had proved difficult it had produced my two biggest from the river that season. I could have returned and fished later into the year but I felt a just reward had been handed out and with the thoughts of a 3lb roach from Willow Pool filling my mind, decided to leave the river alone until the following year.

June the 16th 2007 came, and this year I wanted to relive the days when we had to wait until midnight to cast in. For me, there was only one place I wanted to be; on the Thames, in idyllic surroundings and spending it with my dad. The weather was great and after baiting up, we enjoyed a curry fit for a king, as well as a couple of glasses of red wine. The rods were cast out at midnight and we relaxed. Catching really would just have been a bonus, yet in the early hours one of Dad's rods fished mid-river roared off and after a few anxious moments a hard-fighting, mid-double common graced his net.

The following week, we were back and a repeat performance took place, but this time it was just after dawn when I watched as a powerful fish stripped line off Dad's reel, heading downstream and past the snag. I must admit I wasn't hopeful and as I watched, a branch in the snag started to shake to every turn of Dad's reel. We felt there would be only one winner, yet amazingly, the fish came alongside and instead of diving into the snag, it just kept coming. As I slid the net under her, I instantly recognised the fish as the one that Dad had landed on my rod while I was playing the much sought-after ghostie common, back in 2004. When Dad had landed the fish back then, it had weighed 22lb 5oz and would have been a personal best for him but he didn't want to claim it at the time, so we put it down as a joint effort, yet some three years later, the same fish

had graced his net, and weighing 22lb 6oz became another personal best.

It seemed that Dad was on a roll, yet our next session on July the 19th 2007 coincided with one of the biggest storms and prolonged downpours ever recorded in the country. We hadn't looked at the weather forecast, if we had we wouldn't have ventured out, but we did and shortly after our arrival the rain started. It was relentless, we were confined to our shelters and as dawn broke, the full extent of the damage was obvious. I knew that the river was rising and the fields were flooding but the scene was something I had never witnessed and the decision was made there and then, to get the hell out of what could soon become a dangerous situation.

As I packed the kit away, I heard a bleep and turned to the rods. Surely, it was the flow dislodging the lead, but as I watched, the tip pulled down and I lifted the rod. Half expecting a branch or some other debris to be the problem, I felt a tap on the rod and knew that a carp was hooked but instead of taking it easy, I simply bullied it in until it was under the rod tip and dropped her in the net, yet it wasn't until I lifted the net, that I realised that this carp was massive. Dad came down and as quickly as we could, we lifted her on to the scales and watched as the needle past the 30 mark again, this time coming to rest at 30lb 4oz.

The rain was so bad that Dad took the picture under the cover of my oval and as I slid her back, little did I know that further downstream, the under-equipped sewage plants were struggling to cope with the flood, and I found myself fishing out in a storm that was to pollute the tidal reaches for a second time. It also had a devastating impact on the nature of the river, and although I caught a couple of carp the following year, it was obvious that what these were carp that had escaped from flooded lakes. The swims that had taken us so long to discover had changed, some didn't even produce bream, and I just didn't feel right continuing what had initially started out as a mini-adventure.

The boat still sits in the front garden; the thought of selling it just seems wrong, yet as I write this chapter I'm full of fond memories and with other venues becoming busier by the year, I know that the banks of the Thames will remain relatively neglected, but it's still home to some unknown monsters, and who knows, the old girl might just get a re-launch one day.

Caught as the river broke its banks.

Itchen to get at the ladies

River Itchen

Over the years, Blobby had been an absolute godsend with a wealth of angling knowledge. I had learned not to take anything lightly from him because whatever information he gave was usually reliable. Blobby is a postman, working around the Petersfield area, and while on his round he stumbled upon a once-in-a-lifetime opportunity. He took it with both hands and I thank him unreservedly for sharing it with me.

As he was dropping a household's letters off he noticed a cane salmon rod and wicker basket resting in the corner of a conservatory. The owner had come to the door to collect the mail and Blobby sparked a conversation with him, asking where he fished for salmon, which turned out to be the River Itchen. Being an opportunist, he asked if he could possibly fish the river for species other than salmon. Amazingly, his timing couldn't have been better as other beats on the river had seen an ever-increasing poaching problem and the owner was looking for someone to keep an eye on the stretch during the off-season period. Blobby had gained access to fish a very expensive salmon beat through a brief conversation on someone's doorstep; now that doesn't happen every day!

He was allowed to fish weekdays with maggots only, and any game fish that was accidentally caught had to be released with the minimum of handling, along with being noted in the catch book within the angler's hut that sat on the river bank. Anyone found on the beat while Blobby was fishing had to be reported immediately, but not approached; this would be acted on by means of someone with authority coming straight down to the river with Blobby acting as reinforcement if needed. Even better, he was granted permission to take a guest.

The following words are taken from my diary on the first day that I spent on the venue:
River Itchen, Friday 3rd Oct 2003.

My God! Blobby has just gained rights to fish an exclusive catch-and-release salmon stretch of the River Itchen near Eastleigh for coarse species, once the salmon season has ended. It's music to my ears!

Left home at 4.30am arriving back at 8pm, a lot of effort but what a day's fishing we've just had! Covered the entire beat using the stick float and maggot and managed over 60 grayling during the course of the day plus a bonus brownie that went straight back. At least 50 per cent of the grayling were over the pound mark with many just a few ounces short of our target, a two-pounder, but it was the last fish of the day that achieved this, one of 2lb 4oz 8drams, another nearer 3lb broke me up! Blobby also had a result taking a personal best chub of 4lb 10oz plus a dozen grayling to 1lb 13oz on the tip. What a day, and how will I ever repay this guy.

River low, cold and clear. Weather stayed dry all day even though rain was forecast for the early hours, fairly bright as well with a north-west wind. At least ten salmon spotted, all sitting on round gravel clearings.

Well, that's how it all started, in simply spectacular fashion. Blobby fished the stretch a number of times before I was invited back some two months later, but it was on this occasion that I felt a partnership forming, as although both sociable anglers, when we were actually fishing, we both needed space so we could focus and get the best out of what we had grown up to love, fishing.

That second visit to the stretch was on a very blustery December day. Simply controlling a float was difficult, to say the least, but later in the day, after catching around a dozen grayling, I found some shelter in a swim known as 'DB Fancy' and once again the float disappeared.

The fish was hooked well down the long run and after a brief head shake, which confirmed that it was a grayling, a stalemate was met. Trying to bring the fish up through the fast water on such a tiny hook would have tested it to the limit, so I slowly gained line by moving downstream and guiding what was now obviously a huge grayling into the steadier pool above the boundary swim. After a few anxious moments, she found the bottom of the landing net

and it was then that I realised this might be a three-pounder. Blobby came down to do the honours with the scales and camera and a weight of 2lb 13oz was recorded. Great euphoria followed and as the capture sank in we both realised that we had in our hands a very special piece of fishing, one that was capable of producing a fish of a lifetime; a three-pound grayling.

The following week it was to be Blobby who caught the best fish, matching my best of 2lb 13oz, a different fish taken on the feeder from the Horseshoe Bend.

Brace shots like these were commonplace.

A very special place.

January arrived, as did the storms, and I remember one morning very well. It had been raining all night and the wind had bought the odd tree down. Travelling to the venue was treacherous in itself but it was Blobby's day off and we were going fishing, come what may. The stove was lit in the hut and I recall the wind howling through the delicate poplars above. It wasn't quite light and it was obvious that the river was high, yet not to be beaten Blobby simply slipped his waterproofs on, downed his tea and headed out into the torrential rain and howling wind, leaving me in the hut. It was a this point that I questioned his sanity and could have easily stayed within the shelter of the hut, but I wasn't to be beaten either and knew that if I didn't show the same enthusiasm as Blobby, then I might not be invited back.

After an hour, we sensibly called it a day, biteless. Not only was the river high and coloured but also an oil slick covered the whole river from a spillage upstream and when one of those big wooden seats found in pub gardens came floating past, we knew we were on to a losing battle. We needed another venue and Blobby mentioned a small village pond in South Harting, one that may just hold a 2lb roach. This was more information that my fishing partner had stored away, but these roach didn't show, just massive goldfish, obvious throwaways after funfairs held on the village green.

Being married and having a full time job, Blobby limited himself to just one day a week. Working shifts meant that this would often mean a day off in the week and with me being self-employed, I could easily fit in with his schedule. However, if a session didn't materialise I would either go to Kingfisher Lake, when it was cold, for perch, or head to the Loddon for barbel and chub.

Caught in successive casts.

A brace of specimen grayling.

One thing I learned from Blobby was that a day meant a day, and when we arranged to fish it would mean meeting well before daybreak, travelling down to Eastleigh, sometimes cooking breakfast in the fishing hut, all before the first rays of light had started to illuminate the marshland surrounding the river. The wooden hut was situated smack in the middle of the beat and I would always offer Blobby the choice of which direction to go, to spend the morning, yet a gentleman as always, he insisted on a level playing field and always tossed a coin for this.

The downstream stretch, although shorter, held far more features including named swims such as the Boundary swim, D.B. Fancy, and the Horseshoe Bend, along with the Hut Shallows and Your Swim, both of which we named while spending time on the stretch, and in testimony of just how good they were.

Upstream, there were two small wooden bridges, plenty of shallows, plus a few pools created by the wooden barriers angled into the river, positioned to increase the flow and create a better habitat for the salmon to spawn. The downstream section seemed to hold far fewer fish but these were bigger, yet two of the best swims were influenced by a sewage pipe outfall that on some days would cloud the river and make them almost unfishable.

What was comforting for me was that, if Blobby won the toss and decided to head downstream, something he didn't always do, I knew that he would be fishing the feeder, and even if he fished his heart out in each swim, there would always be scope for me on the float to tempt a few more later in the day.

We complemented each other's fishing. We were both extremely organised so that we hardly ever had to borrow anything from each other. If we did catch up during the day, it would be to have lunch in the hut, after which we'd swap over and cover the ground already fished by the other. Sometimes, one of us might have landed a big fish and needed a photograph taken; something that became common on this stretch.

Although we tried our best to fish the stretch as often as we could until the end of the season, we only managed another four trips, yet the grayling fishing was always superb and it was commonplace to catch 40 or more grayling each in a day,

many of which were over 2lb. Chub were also becoming more common; one day I took seven to 4lb 9oz after locating a shoal, whipping them into a feeding frenzy by regular introductions of maggots before casting a line and extracting the vast majority.

Lunchtime was always fun as we would discuss the events of the previous hours, and it was on one such occasion that Blobby decided to cast his feeder out into probably no more than a foot of water. What happened next surprised us both, as soon after doing so, the tip started to bounce and the first of what was to be numerous 2lb grayling graced his net. It happened so often that it became a joke and I remember him taking three two-pounders, only for a friend to turn up, cast out and catch his first-ever grayling, one that weighed 2lb 10oz!

Blobby's spot was outside the hut.

It wasn't just grayling that gave us new personal bests!

Our last session that season was on March the 8th and it was a day I would never forget. I arrived in near-perfect conditions and after winning the toss I headed downstream. The overcast conditions were great for float fishing and with not so much as a breath of wind I would be able to control the float easily and long trot many a swim. I also created a game plan where I would feed a swim, catch four fish from it, feed again then move. I hoped this would not spook and kill a swim and that I could return later for a few more.

The plan seemed to work and it was while in My Swim, a swim so called because no one apart from me seemed to be able to catch from it, that a big fish was once again hooked. This fish was in a league of its own, staying deep, and all I could do was to keep the pressure on until she slowly tired. It was then that the she decided to exit the pool and head upstream, tail-walking as she went. Luck was on my side this day, and although she seemed more in control than me for most of the fight, she finally succumbed to the pressure.

Blobby had witnessed the fight from the Horseshoe Bend and was making his way down, and when he saw me punch the air, his stride quickened in anticipation. This grayling was huge and on the scales we watched as the dial swung round, finally settling bang on 3lb. That day can only be considered a red-letter day and I went on to land another two more 2lb grayling, with Blobby taking four over the magical mark; his biggest was 2lb 9oz.

Looking through my dairy, I think we took no fewer than 20 grayling over 2lb that season, finally achieving what was considered an impossible feat, and from a stretch of river we were really just discovering. When the season ended we just couldn't wait for October to come again. Late spring and early summer was spent between a number of waters, the highlight being the capture of a 37lb 4oz catfish taken on a plug after dark, plus a few eel sessions, yet the amount of captures didn't really justify the hours spent on the bank. Unexpectedly, we were granted permission to fish our special stretch of the Itchen far sooner than we had expected the following season, July in fact, probably due to a spate of vandalism which had seen every other angling hut torched, except for ours.

Straightaway, we noticed an increase in the numbers of grayling, yet most were small and from two visits nearly 200 grayling were caught, but just two surpassed the 2lb mark. I think that although it was great to be able to fish the river during the summer, we both felt that it was really a winter retreat; it was also a period when I was getting into carp fishing on the Thames with my father, so it wasn't surprising that we both waited until September to return.

A very big pike had been reported in the stretch and knowing that it had done a 30 in the past, and after being allowed by the owner, Blobby wasted no time in packing a pike rod. The grayling fishing, although good, wasn't what we had become to expect, however, Blobby managed three double-figure pike to 14lb on our first trip back, but the monster couldn't be found.

A dream come true is a 3lb grayling.

161

An ounce under six pounds from the Itchen.

Blobby's love for the river was dwindling, why I'm not sure, but I remember him saying that the fishing was very predictable and apart from the grayling and chub, he needed something different to captivate his mind. Luckily, he spoke with the owner who agreed that I could take his place, so with Blobby's interests elsewhere, I found myself able to take a guest, and who better than Dad.

It was a perfect situation; we didn't have to rush because no one else would be on the river, parking was secure and right next to the hut, plus we had the amenities to make hot drinks throughout the day and the fishing was simply fantastic.

Our first visit was one to be remembered. Although we had seen numerous salmon while fishing the beat, no one had actually hooked one, but that was all to

change as while guiding Dad, he went and hooked one. It was really touch and go stuff and I remember doing no favours to Dad's nerves as I was a total mess trying to land the fish. Finally, in she went and as Dad lifted his 6lb 13oz salmon, I remember thinking, 'this is just pure paradise'.

Blobby still occasionally came and continued to use the feeder, something I refused to do, as it was often the case that deep hooking would occur and with grayling being so delicate, I felt that it just wasn't right. I recall one occasion when I spotted a big grayling that had moved into the edge of the Horseshoe Bend, yet as hard as I tried I could not tempt it by using float tactics. Blobby arrived and dropped his feeder next to the grayling and it simply moved toward his static bait, sucked in the hookbait and the fish was duly extracted. Bingo!

This fish weighed 2lb 2oz and from watching this event I realised just how effective yet dangerous feeder tactics are, as not the slightest of indication registered through the rod tip. My float skills had improved considerably while fishing the stretch, yet I was still using an open face reel and annoyingly was still losing probably 30 per cent of hooked fish, most immediately after clicking the bail arm over. It was a frustrating situation, something that I had lived with until now due to just enjoying the fantastic fishing, but deep down I knew that I had to buy a centrepin if I were to solve the problem.

The following words are taken from my diary of a red-letter session in October:

River Itchen, Sunday 3rd Oct 2004.

The river's cold and clear with a brisk easterly wind blowing and clear blue skies. Started on the Horseshoe Bend as a large grayling was on the gravel drop-off but after numerous small grayling on the float it refused to take my maggot hookbait. Blobby arrived and lowered a feeder next to it and seconds later landed it at 2lb 2oz. I decided to rotate swims, catching three or four fish from each before feeding, and moving to the next, feeding the others on the way.

This tactic worked and I continuously caught grayling from them all, but no monsters, up to around 1lb 8oz. Grayling were present under the small bush above Your Swim but the wind made it difficult to fish, yet first trot through saw a good fish hooked. Twenty minutes later my first-ever salmon of 6lb 10oz graced my net. A few more grayling came before a move back to the run into the main bend saw another good fish hooked.

The personal best's kept falling.

Sea trout spent most of the time out of the water when hooked.

After another long battle a salmon of 5lb 9oz was landed. Alternating between these swims saw lots more grayling landed before lunch, along with taking photographs of a 2lb grayling for Blobby who had added a 1lb 14oz 8dram specimen from the shallows in front of the hut, while I made my way up to him.

I decided to try the Boundary swim that had proven hard for Blobby earlier that day due to the sewage entering the river. First trot down and another powerful fish is hooked that fought as much out of the water as in! This was identified eventually as a sea trout of 7lb 7oz. A few brown trout followed before my first 2lb grayling was landed from the rushes at the end of the beat, 2lb 2oz. D.B. Fancy was next on my list and the first fish was a grayling of 2lb 9oz. A small sea trout plus grayling and trout followed between the swims before another sea trout of 6lb 1oz was netted. A trot through the rushes saw a good sea trout lost as it tail-walked down the

rapids into the lower section. It was now late afternoon and content with my catch I returned to the bend. A few maggots over the drop-off saw a salmon and good chub become active. Tackle retied and first cast a chub was hooked that turned the scales to 5lb 15oz! Four personal bests in one session; it doesn't get much better.

The next few months were enjoyed spending time with my father who, being a traditionalist, persisted with the float and come mid-December finally landed his first-ever 2lb grayling. In fact, on this particular day he landed two, weighing 2lb 4oz and 2lb 1oz, along with a personal best chub of 4lb 6oz.

Captures of salmon became commonplace. However, although I caught on most visits, in all the hours that Blobby put in on the river he failed to catch one, even after trying the float through certain productive swims. It was also a time when I seemed inundated with offers to join me, and most of my guests managed to catch grayling over the 2lb mark.

It came as no surprise when my parent bought me a centrepin. It was a birthday present and one that I couldn't wait to try out. Although frustrating at first, over time my skills improved and soon I was trotting a line perfectly and when a bite came all that was needed to set the hook was to press my finger on the drum and flick my wrist.

The winter weather was also proving to be a testing time. London had reported snow falling for 11 days on the trot, yet grayling feed in the cruellest of conditions and although travelling to the river was sometimes treacherous, we still managed to make regular visits. That winter I landed 32 grayling over 2lb, the biggest 2lb 11oz and I think it was a combination of better float control as well as using sweetcorn towards the back end of the season that boosted my results.

The centrepin had injected new life into my river fishing but just as Blobby had felt the previous year, my enthusiasm and excitement for the river was dwindling. It was as if there were no surprises left to be discovered,

or so I thought, as on the last session I spotted two massive perch.

They were obviously in a spawning ritual with the biggest well over 4lb. I tried everything to tempt them, even resorting to lying on the ground and bouncing a worm on their noses while holding the line from my hands. How they ignored this, I will never know.

Those perch kept me interested but as for the grayling, sometimes you can get too much of a good thing and when the season finished I was almost relieved. I needed some diversity and the spring and summer certainly brought that.

Salmon or sea trout? I'm guessing a salmon!

Marsh Farm's crucians were discovered, as were the silver bream at Mill Farm Fishery, which concluded in the capture of my second British record. I paid back my good friend, Blobby, by letting him take a 30lb carp from under my nose at Westhampnett, but it was the time spent with my father targeting carp on the river Thames that stole the show.

October 2005 saw sewage pollution affecting the river and although this entered at the bottom of the beat, it seemed to kill almost everything, even upstream. From three visits my father and I caught just 12 fish, mostly pencil grayling, one of exactly 2lb, a perch, plus two trout, with the chub completely missing.

We decided to give the river a miss for a few months and give it time for it to recover, and as the winter progressed the fishing started to improve, yet long gone were the days of catching 60 grayling, with 12 now being good. The chub also made a return and on one day I managed seven to over 5lb-plus, and a

Pike gave the beat some diversity.

couple of 2lb grayling, but this was a one-off, and in general we struggled for bites.

The spring of 2006 saw me perfecting a method on Marsh Farm and taking some startling captures as well as returning to Westhampnett where it showed its true potential, and as for the Thames carp, they just kept coming, only this time they were bigger!

In 2006, the news came through that the fishery was up for sale so our time looked destined to come to an abrupt end, something that finally happened mid-December that year. My father and I managed six outings before this happened and although the fishing had vastly improved, many of the bigger grayling were repeat captures and out of eight twos that were caught, I think they were made up of three different fish. One very big fish had evaded capture, being lost by both Kevin and Dad.

I was there when Dad lost it and I remember watching it drop back to a spot in the river where I tried getting it to feed again. Literally, hundreds of maggots passed this fish's nose, yet all that day it refused to feed. No angler in the world would have tempted that grayling, not even by using the finest of tackle, and as I watched it I realised that this grayling wasn't just a two-pounder, but it could well be over three!

The following day, I was back and a quick look into the swim showed that she was still there. A few maggots upstream came trickling past her and I watched as she turned and twisted, devouring them all. Not wanting to be under-gunned, I tied a size 12 micro-barbed hook to a 4lb hooklink, shotted the loafer float in the swim upstream, with a bulk and two droppers, and then set the float on course in her direction, along with half a dozen maggots. Sure enough, as the float approached where she sat, it disappeared and by the way the rod bent over I knew exactly which fish I had hooked.

Once again, I allowed her to sit in the current for a while and then as I felt her tiring I slowly made my way down to her, then as I had done once before in the same swim, I guided her into the deeper water of the pool below where she was finally landed. With trembling hands I lifted her on the scales, half expecting the needle to fly past the 3lb mark but it wasn't to be, yet at 2lb 14oz it was my second-biggest from the beat.

December the 14th was our last day on the beat and both me and my father held mixed emotions, as we knew that we had fished a stretch of river in its prime, and then witnessed its decline.

It's strange but often in my angling career I have seemed to catch a special fish, either at the last knockings of a session, or the last day on a venue and today was to be no exception as after an explosive fight, we slipped the net under a salmon, far bigger than those previously taken and weighed 12lb 1oz. It seemed a fitting way to say goodbye.

My final fling with the ladies was over, and no longer was I Itchen to get at them.

Plugging at night
Badshot Lea

I've always tried to catch certain species by design. Don't get me wrong, I will accept an accidental capture with open arms but it gives me far more satisfaction when rigs, location and bait application have been adapted to suit the species. It was this mentality that saw me trying something completely different, angling pioneering some may say, and the species I had in mind was catfish.

Farnham Angling Society's Badshot Lea Big Pond was the destination and having grown up fishing this lake, I had seen it evolve from a large, windswept, natural environment to a comfortable, accommodating fishery. Personally, I loved the early days when it was far more natural than the commercial feel it creates now, but what it lacked in the early days was variety, something that you certainly couldn't fault it for today.

In 1994, wels catfish were introduced, around a hundred as I recall, and still being interested in pike fishing this new species created an interesting diversion through the summer months. At first these cats could easily be targeted by design and the favourite bait back then was squid, which on occasions brought multiple catches, even during daylight.

The following year, another stocking took place, when around 180lb of cats weighing between three and six pounds were introduced. Slowly, the fishery became more and more popular, the maintenance around the lake, especially swim construction was making it accommodating to the longer stay angler and the fish within it were growing.

The increased introduction of pellets and boilies soon saw the catfish in the lake change their feeding habits and although they could still be occasionally caught on specific baits, it became more and more common to watch a carp angler land a couple of cats on fishmeal boilies, while the squid went unnoticed. It was frustrating; targeting cats by design became increasingly harder and for a few years I decided not to target them. However, the boilie, especially Activ-8, proved its effectiveness and became the downfall of numerous cats to 26lb 4oz.

The spring of 2004 arrived, and knowing that my best catfish wasn't taken by design, I needed to change this. The catfish within the lake had grown considerably and 30s and 40s weren't uncommon, so with this in mind I decided to give it another go.

Using squid again was an option, as was live baiting, but my confidence in the first was already knocked, and live baiting is a method I will only use when everything else fails. I was convinced that catfish will always have a predatory instinct, even if their main diet has changed and the thought of lure fishing flashed through my brain. At the time, Fox had just released a new range of lures, so I decided to purchase a selection and try these out, yet during daylight hours all they produced were numerous pike.

Gradually, the day sessions progressed into darkness, a period of great excitement, as the thought of hooking a big cat at night on a lure was just incredible. The use of trebles had also become a problem and it wasn't uncommon to foul hook other species, especially bream, and a conservation-minded decision was made to remove the trebles, replacing them with big singles that reduced the probability of this considerably.

My pioneering hadn't gone unnoticed and soon Kevin and Donut were joining me, but after numerous dark, evening sessions and plenty of pike we still hadn't tempted a catfish.

The following words are taken from my diary:
Badshot Lea Big Pond, Monday 26th April 2004.

Arrived to find most of the lake's carp and bream spawning. Peg 39 is free, so Kevin and I doubled up. Weather's still warm with a gentle south-west wind and thunderstorms and rain have been forecast for later in the week.

Kevin managed a rare tench but it soon became apparent that it was going to be tough as most fish had other things on their minds. I decided to try the plug, and thank God I did, as just on darkness and after a couple of pike, I had a hit from a cat. After a ten-minute fight, a monster of 37lb 4oz lay at the bottom of my net.

We continued into the night taking another pike, a foul-hooked bream, plus two more cats. Kevin's was 12lb 2oz and mine 9lb. Kevin tried the plug at first light and unfortunately, pulled out of another big cat. The liners continued throughout the night to the extent that I reeled both rods in.

Angling pioneering completed.

It just has to happen.

I remember that night so well. It was a night of sheer excitement, as up to that moment I had clocked up nearly 200 hours plug fishing, it was also when a hunch became reality.

The take from the cat can only be described as winding in and hitting a brick wall. I was using powerful gear at the time, a 2.75lb carp rod with 28lb braid and as darkness fell and I looked out into the lake, I remember seeing this massive tail slapping the surface as a stalemate was met. The capture was reported to the weeklies and on further investigation I found out that only one other known bigger catfish in the country had been caught on a lure.

After that evening, we continued to try to tempt more cats but that night seem to be a one-off, one when the catfish's predatory instincts were aroused from the commotion of spawning fish. Our pioneering finally stopped abruptly when the club banned the use of two hooks. Unbeknown to them, we had all already taken steps to protect their fish stocks, yet the ban also stated that only one hook could be used and having completed the task and now being greatly disadvantaged, we moved on.

Carters Hill and Stanford End
River Loddon

Although having fished the river Loddon at Carters Hill and Sindlesham for many years, it was on the 24th November 2004 that the potential of this river was revealed. I had dropped into one of my favourite swims which had a large oak extending across the water.

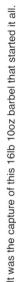

It was the capture of this 16lb 10oz barbel that started it all.

personal best of 10lb 15oz taken the previous season from the Kennet at Burghfield.

It was while chatting that the tip pulled round again, only this time I found myself attached to something far heavier, yet by the lack of a powerful first run, I was unsure whether it was actually a barbel or a carp. The fish stayed deep and I watched as strands of weed, which were being uprooted, floated downstream. It was when a huge barbel surfaced that my legs went to jelly and I recall stretching out my landing net, which was seriously inadequate for landing such a long fish, only for it to flick its tail in defiance and head off downstream.

This provided plenty of shade and although not noted as a barbel swim, it usually provided a chub or two. I had spent a few minutes in a couple of other swims without any joy, so when the rod tip tapped and then pulled round I was happy to find myself playing a fish, which, as expected, turned out to be a 4lb 10oz chub.

My standard practice when roving the river is to move after a capture, however on this particular occasion an angler had passed me a few moments before catching the chub and not wanting to give away another of my baited areas, I chanced another cast. Ten minutes passed and the angler returned only this time he sat down beside me to try to find out a little about the barbel in the stretch. I remember explaining that although I had fished the river for years, most barbel had been caught accidentally and that I was trying to increase my

The run sapped the fish's energy and Dan was now on landing duty because I knew that it would need to be bundled into the small net. When she surfaced again, Dan managed to scoop my prize and as we looked down into the mesh, we were speechless because something very special was lying within the folds. Dan estimated the weight and when he said '15', I looked at him in amazement; a 15lb barbel out of this stretch? Never! After zeroing the scales, we placed her in the sling and Dan lifted her, it was then that I saw the needle travel past 15, then 16, finally settling on 16lb 10oz. It was a fish of a lifetime and a personal best that remains today.

Although this stretch of the Loddon had never produced a barbel anywhere near as big, lower down, below Sindlesham Mill it had, a known fish that regularly visited the bank, one that at its top weight to my knowledge was 15lb 15oz.

Rumours were that my barbel was the same fish and that a couple of anglers had moved it upstream due to it being caught so often, yet I remember removing the hook from the 16 and commenting on how the mouth curtain was still intact. Now, a fish that gets caught so regularly would have lost this long ago, so

I dismissed the rumour. This wasn't the same fish, but one that had very rarely, if ever, been caught before.

However, this barbel did get caught again; in fact, it was caught just two days later, some half a mile downstream by Dan, the same angler who had landed it for me, at two ounces lighter. Amazingly, I was also fishing and returned the favour of taking the photographs, which had to be better than the ones he took for me. Less than a month later, she visited the bank again, close to where I had taken her initially. I was on landing duties this time as she was attached to Kevin's line.

Kevin with the big girl, this time weighing 15lb 12oz.

Here are the actual words taken from my diary:

River Loddon - Carters Hill, Thursday 16th December 2004.

What a river this is becoming. Kevin's got a couple of hours this evening so we decided to meet bankside. I arrived slightly earlier and had primed three swims. The plan was that we would both fish a swim for an hour before meeting and doubling up for a social in the remaining swim. We both caught a couple of chub in our first swims, which is a result on such a tough venue, before meeting at 5pm. Kevin fished the inside crease while I cast over to the far bank.

A chub came to my rod along with a missed chance before Kevin landed two barbel in quick succession. The first was his second-biggest ever, weighing 9lb 12oz, a new fish. The second was the big girl, considerably down in weight at 15lb 12oz but still looking magnificent. A fantastic brace but I just hope she disappears now until March.

This fish started to attract some attention and although I never experienced a mega influx of anglers, the odd new face was beginning to be seen. Two anglers were even spotted with a copy of Angler's Mail and were trying to pinpoint the swim I caught it from by using my photograph.

Typical double that fell to the method-lead during daylight.

The rest of that winter, I regularly fished the stretch, always in my normal roving approach where I would drop a bait into a swim, leave for 40 minutes, and then move on. If I were lucky to catch a fish sooner, whether it be a carp, barbel, chub or bream then I would move, covering ground much quicker while learning the river, and if time allowed I would try the odd new area. Some would ask why I didn't stay in a swim that I'd had caught from, but I had tried this on many occasion, rarely getting another chance so had adapted a mobile approach that suited my short sessions. I had also found that if any fish were in a swim then bites would come quickly, quite often within five minutes, so by visiting a number of swims I was able to up my catch rate considerably.

I had also tried fishing into dark, yet even before trying this I knew I wouldn't enjoy it, as I had spent many an evening watching an isotope in previous years, below Sindlesham Mill, often falling asleep and rarely seeing an increase in bites. So it was day fishing for me, and with my mobile approach I managed to fish all the swims I needed to, catch plenty, and then leave well before anyone else arrived. It was a devastating tactic that saw numerous barbel grace my net that winter, the pick of the bunch being a 13lb 3oz beard that fell on the 31st December.

The following season arrived and being well into my carp fishing on the Thames I finally went back to the banks of Carters late in October. The weed was still a major problem and by the look of some of the swims we weren't going to be alone as some were worn quite heavily. Carters has never been easy, especially for

The first part of Dad's fantastic brace.

An unforgettable brace.

barbel and getting a bite of any description was classified as a result, so when I found myself heading home after a four-hour spell in which six swims were covered, with a 6lb bream to my name, I was happy. Four further trips produced fish on every occasion, yet it wasn't until the fourth, in December, that the tip pulled round in all too familiar barbel fashion. Weighing 10lb 12oz it was a repeat capture from the previous winter but it had put on 1lb 8oz, and I started to realise that if this was a standard weight gain for a barbel here, then we could have some colossal fish in front of us.

Another barbel to the method-lead.

The number of anglers was increasing, probably due to the publicity it was getting and most headed for the deep water above the bridge, one I had called Cyanide Straight. Luckily, it's an area I rarely fish, preferring the long walk, and that winter I was rewarded with another big barbel weighing 13lb 2oz.

The next remarkable session was on the 19th of January 2006, when Dad joined me. It was at the end of a mild spell and with a period of cold weather forecast to hit the country. I placed Dad in the swim that I had taken the big girl from as I knew he would get a chance, even if it was from a chub, yet less than half an hour had

passed when I saw him making his way upstream. A big smile said it all as in his landing net lay a very big barbel, and weighing 12lb 5oz it recorded a new personal best.

Back in my swim, I finally got a bait into position only for the tip to pull round but after a brief fight I found myself licking my wounds, as the hooklink had parted. Allowing Dad to move around saw me sitting tight for a couple of hours but with little showing I made my way back downstream, eventually sitting next to Dad who was in a new swim and he mentioned that he'd missed a couple of bites.

'They can't have been barbel', I thought, and as we watched his tip tremble, then pull round, I remember shouting, 'strike!' This he did, which saw the clutch scream as a big fish headed off downstream. Locked in battle, I wondered whether this could be the big girl come to reward all the anglers in the Charman household, and as she went into the net I was still wondering. On the mat, we could see clearly that this was indeed a new fish and a big one at that, and weighing 13lb 12oz rewarded Dad with another best

and an unforgettable brace. Little did we know at the time that this brace would see Dad invited to the Southern Angler Species Final at Pallatrax Lakes, a match that saw him win £1000!

The following winter, I only visited Carters twice. The reason was that I had been allocated a syndicate place on the famous Willow Pool on the Lynch Hill Complex and having the fantastic grayling fishing on the River Itchen, found my time channelled elsewhere.

This stunner regularly visited the bank, weighing between 15lb 5oz and 16lb 1oz.

The winter of 2008 was different though, and after witnessing what I call 'syndicate swim stitch up' I was glad to be back on home soil. Unbeknown to me, the season before, two very capable anglers had decided to give Carters a good going over and had, after they had finished with the stretch, decided to make their catches known to all, or almost. I remember an angler approaching me on my first trip to Carters and muttering the words, "Oh, you're obviously here to catch the 20."

To be honest, I had lost touch with Carters, but on further investigation it seemed that two different very big barbel had been caught on the same evening the previous season, and rumours of a 20 were circulating the grapevine. He wasn't the only barbel angler around, there were three, all set up with two rods in the deep straight above the bridge, and with another one making his way across the fields, I knew that things were going to be different.

Travelling light, I headed upstream, well away from the glory seekers and had planned to make my way downstream, searching different swims out until I received a bite, yet I wasn't expecting a bite quite as quickly as it came, for just ten minutes after settling in the top swim the tip wrapped around and an 11-pounder found its way into the waiting net. I smiled once more as over the previous winters I had created a method that rarely let me down in the autumn months - the method-lead. It's a method that was chanced on many years before, again while fishing the Loddon, this time further downstream around Sindlesham Mill.

This is what I remember of the night when PVA was forgotten and I caught my first Loddon barbel by design using the 'method-lead':

It was a wild afternoon when I arrived, with high winds and rain forecast but extremely mild, perfect for barbel. Friends had been catching their fair share of barbel including the odd double, yet I was struggling, so decided to venture out. Blanking wasn't an option. I remember telling the girlfriend that I wasn't coming home until one graced my net; it was a challenge and I was up for it.

Hours passed, as did plenty of good-looking swims, yet still the rod tip failed to move. I was using PVA bags of pellets at the time, which were attached to the hook with a 13mm hard pellet on the hair. I had made up around a dozen and by the time I started to run out it was getting on for midnight. The wind had increased and the rain began to fall, so I placed the rod on the ground, tip pointing skywards, as we all did back then, and proceeded to tie up a few spare bags before the rain got too bad, but halfway through the bag tying process, the rod whacked round, lifting the butt off the ground.

In a mad panic, I grabbed for the rod, missing it in the process and sending pellets and PVA in all directions. Completely gutted, I remember sitting with my head in my hands for a few minutes as I tried to regain some sort of composure. Winding in, I placed the rod on the rest and started to pick the pellets off the ground as best I could. They were all wet and I recall thinking, 'these are sticky', so placed them in a bait box and added some hot tea out of my flask. A few minutes passed before I found I could mould these around the lead and cast out without having to use expensive PVA. I also realised that by doing this, my feed was above the hookbait, so if it attracted anything then the chance of my hookbait being taken first was high.

Two swims later, the pellets were even stickier and as I made an underarm cast I felt everything touch bottom with a satisfying thud. Holding the rod, I almost knew the outcome and moments later found myself playing a Loddon barbel at long last, caught by design.

Since that fateful day, I can count on one hand the times I've used PVA when barbel fishing, and the method-lead is as good today as it was then.

The 11-pounder was just the start I needed, and along with a couple of modest chub I left a happy man, knowing that Carters would be good to me that winter. Although there was an influx of anglers, regular faces were rare, as most newcomers soon found out just how tough it could be.

I just had to return at dawn; my prize, a 16lb 1oz barbel.

A regular visitor to the bank.

Steve Fantauzzi and Steve Wybourn were two regulars and the three of us soon respected each other's space, catching up for a quick chat as one or the other left. Both these anglers were rovers, anglers that used just one rod and searched out the river, just as I did, so if I arrived and found one of their cars parked up, I would simply find where they were, then give them at least ten swims either side. It was a system that worked really well, especially knowing that I would normally fish the daylight hours up till dusk, Steve Fantauzzi would arrive after work and fish a few hours into dark and the other Steve was nocturnal, arriving after dark and fishing right through to dawn.

Using pellet, my approach seem to work well up to the start of the New Year and it was rare that a barbel wouldn't be landed from each session. However, once the New Year arrived my barbel results started to tumble, but chub were still obliging. That winter I landed 27 barbel, including two 15s and a new fish that seem to live well upstream, she weighed 16lb 7oz.

Steve Fantauzzi's barbel results started to increase in the cold weather, probably down to him having introduced his boilie over a few months and now that the pellet was losing its edge, he found the barbel queuing up. Another factor is that he's just an absolutely brilliant angler, and it came as no surprise to hear that he had just landed one of the big girls, at an all-time high of 19lb 2oz!

Steve Wybourn quite often used an altogether different approach and rolled meat, even after dark. I'm not too sure on his results, but without a doubt he was top rod in terms of numbers and I seem to recall him saying that he had landed over 70 barbel one winter, 30 of these being repeat captures, so in my earlier predictions on numbers of barbel through this stretch, he had caught nearly all of them, including Steve's 19.

I did come close to landing what I think was one of the two big barbel in the stretch. With two days to go before the season ended, I found myself tucked in a swim known as the Rocks. The river was up, coloured and raging through, and with a nasty snag downstream I knew that if I hooked a fish then this would probably come into play in such conditions. Sure enough, the rod wrenched round and I found myself locked in battle with a big fish. As it started to head downstream, I had only one option and that was to slow it down by clamping my hand around the spool. It seemed to work as the fish lifted in the water, yet disaster was looming. Just as the fish surfaced and I thought the battle was won, the rod sprang back and she was gone, leaving me on my backside.

The following year, my results were similar with the pellet working its wonders until the end of the year and, once again, the odd big fish appeared. I remember an angler stopping me and politely asking me for some tips on catching, as he had spent numerous sessions on the stretch without a bite. My advice was simple, 'go for the long walk and find areas away from others'. This he did and when we next met, he thanked me as he had landed a couple of fish, the best an 11-pounder.

It was this same angler who passed me one evening and asked if he could settle in the swim above me. I had absolutely no problem with this as on a previous session I'd had a lead around in it, only to find it rather snaggy, and had always given it a wide berth since that day. Amazingly, out went his rod and in came a 7lb barbel and on quizzing him I found that this swim had been quite kind to him.

Settling back in my position, a feeling came flooding through me. It was one that I remembered while pike fishing through the stretch on the odd occasion in the past, and it was a feeling that rarely let me down. It was as if the river was talking to me, and it was telling me to go home and return at first light, and to settle in the swim where this angler was.

The following morning, I was back, just before daybreak. I remember vividly, struggling to watch the rod tip in the growing light of the sky, when suddenly it was gone and my arm was being ripped off. To be honest, I piled on the pressure and almost pumped the barbel across the river, knowing full well what sat out of sight a few yards downstream. Luck was with me this time, and I watched as a good barbel came across the landing net.

It wasn't just barbel that were caught.

Still unaware of its true size, I switched on my head torch and shone it down. It was then I realised that, sitting in my net was a fish I should have given far more respect to, but if I had I might not have found out what it was. On the scales the needle settled, and once again a new fish had appeared, this time weighing 16lb 1oz. It was a fish that was to become quite friendly from then on, and along with the sixteen taken from roughly the same area the previous year, graced my net on numerous occasions. In fact, it came to the point that I decided to leave this area alone and headed downstream below the bridge, as these, plus other recaptures including carp, made me think that I had caught most of its inhabitants.

Below the bridge was far more challenging, with numerous snags where the barbel could hold up, but one swim did produce regularly. It was a deep drop-off, probably the best pike swim on the whole river, yet although the odd barbel was caught from it, more often than not a bream or chub would ruin your chances.

One memorable night was when I decided to try using boilies as bait. Steve Fantauzzi was using the same and had mentioned that he wasn't getting pestered by chub so I thought I would try them out. However, 12 swims later and with 12 chub landed, I started to question if he was telling me porkies! The thirteenth swim, though, did produce a barbel.

It was a rare occasion when I had taken a second rod, things were getting that tough, and had cast an 18mm boilie upstream, as the swim allowed for this. It was strange as upstream fishing was new to me and I remember the tip dropping back violently before the rod was almost pulled in. Weighing 13lb 3oz I watched as she leaked copious amounts of white maggots over my hand as I lifted her for a photo, and then started to think about who would be using maggot. What's more, the maggots seemed to be in different stages of breakdown, some new, some old, so these were being introduced regularly. The other thing that struck me was that I was fishing just below the bridge and saw no established swims, which made me think that this fish was on the move, travelling up from the snags to feed in the deep straight, an area where most people fished.

I quizzed young Steve on whether he was using maggots, something he denied, and then asked why I was being trashed by chub on the same bait that he was using, while all he was catching was barbel, only to be told that his boilie maker had removed a product from his batch that deterred the chub from eating them. Is this possible? I still smile and wonder if Steve's wonder bait was maggots. Only he knows and I can speculate.

The event of that barbel leaking maggots all over me didn't go to waste, though, as I relayed my findings to my father, only for him to visit the river a week later, cast out a homemade inline maggot feeder and extract a new personal best barbel weighing 14lb 4oz. Acting on something, whether told or seen, is obviously something I have inherited and can only thank my father for this, as like him, I'm not one to sit and wonder.

My biggest eel caught from running water.

This fortunate attribute was bought home earlier in the year when visiting my dad and Kevin who were once again fishing the Loddon, as after talking to them I headed upstream and watched as another angler lost a very big eel. Two days later I was back and proceeded to land my biggest eel from running water, an event that can be read in my chapter on eels.

The capture of that big eel the previous year saw me returning during the height of summer. A quick lead around located just two swims that I felt confident presenting a bait, the weed was that bad. Numerous nights were spent in search of another monster snake, but although eels to 4lb 5oz graced my net it was one I lost that I will never forget.

Here are the words taken from my diary of that night:

River Loddon - Carters Hill, Wednesday 4th August 2010.

Conditions: Showers clearing, leaving a cool night with lows of 12 degrees and atmospherics of 1014mb, wind from the north-west.
Duration of session: Overnight.
Tactics: Lobworms during darkness for eels and pellet in the daylight for barbel.
Result: One 2lb eel, plus a very big one lost after biting through 25lb Quicksilver, plus two barbel weighing 12lb 11oz on the worms and 13lb 3oz on pellet, plus a 5lb 4oz chub.

Dad, with his maggot-caught 14lb 4oz barbel.

That session was never repeated, and if I had landed that big eel, just think of the write-up in the press! Looking back, I wish I had persisted multi-species targeting on the Loddon, but the effort of lugging all the kit across the fields was taking its toll. It was an amazing fish, and one that has me returning each year to see if it can be bettered, however, to date, the best I have taken is 4lb 10oz.

This capture reminds me of another situation that I found myself in during the summer of 2010. It was a warm July afternoon and I had settled in a swim under a couple of big willows. The reason for this was, unlike the rest of the river that was choked in weed, the shade from the trees had prevented any growth and I was able to place baits without the fear of them being masked. The trees, however, made it

Caught while multi-targeting different species.

impossible to set up close to the rods and I found myself a few feet away from them.

Around 7am, I was awoken by my alarm screaming and rushed to the rod, but as I picked this up, my momentum, plus the pull of a hard-fighting barbel, and me tripping on the banksticks of my second rod that I hadn't removed, saw me doing a somersault into the river. The rod was dropped, ending up in the river and I can honestly say that I think I wasn't properly awake until fully submerged.

Opening my eyes, all I could see was the colour of tea and frantically struggled to get my head above the surface. It was then that panic kicked in. My overalls were double-lined and were filling up with water and I remember feeling really heavy and out of my depth but luckily, I made it to the bank where I struggled to get out.

Shivering and down to my underpants, I wonder if anyone spotted me as I pushed my trolley over the mist-covered fields. Taking into consideration that I wasn't wearing any shoes or thick jumpers, I still struggled to get out and that worries me to this day. I still find it difficult to fish after dark on flowing water, especially in the winter.

My attentions were also focusing on another stretch run by Farnham Angling Society, further upstream at Stanford End, and as I was looking at beginning a guiding service for the angler, I knew that Carters would just be too tough. My first pupil on the stretch was my dad, and although he was well aware of the catching properties of the method-lead, I spent an afternoon with him perfecting his approach.

Twice that day, the tip wrapped round, resulting in barbel of 8lb and 10lb 13oz. It was a great day spent chatting and from that moment on I knew that helping other anglers catch fish of their dreams was what I was destined to do. I was also lucky enough to catch the biggest barbel in the stretch, twice, weighing 14lb 14oz and 15lb 3oz so it was a great month in my angling career.

I was also fortunate to spend a day on the bottom stretch of Stratford Saye, producing a film for Coarse and Match Fishing Monthly. It was an eventful day, firstly as cameraman, John Dunsford, and I crouched as the biggest bull we had ever seen strolled past just a few feet from where we were sitting and then later managing to catch two chub, one that decided to deposit a digested crayfish from its vent onto my arm, as well as a last-minute barbel.

Here are the words taken from my diary of that session:
River Loddon, Tuesday 10th August 2010.

Coarse and Match Monthly 'The Session'.
Conditions: Wet, rain all day with temperatures between 13 and 19 degrees. A n/w wind and atmospherics of 1008mb.
Duration of session: 9-30am until 4-30pm.
Tactics: Roving around for barbel with the method-lead and pellet.
Result: Two big chub of 5lb 1oz and 6lb 1oz plus a last cast barbel of 12lb!

Caught a few weeks later at 14lb 14oz.

As for Carters, I stayed away during the autumn and winter of 2010 as much of my time was spent targeting other species, such as perch. Although I have to admit to loving Carters, it's not a place that I miss. I think that by spending so many hours on its bank over so many years, I've grown to understand how it ticks and although years can be missed, I always feel that when I return, I can quickly tune into the way it behaves, and knowing the swims intimately, soon get a result.

The winter of 2011 was no exception, and although I spent very little time at Carters, the time I did find myself on its bank wasn't wasted. Some anglers had almost given their lives to targeting those two big fish and one mentioned how he had spent over 20 nights without a fish! I headed downstream that evening and within two hours was lifting a 12lb barbel up for a photo and on further visits caught more.

Static or mobile, pellet or boilie, night or day, it's really up to the individual, yet for me, if I do the same as everyone else, then my results are going to be similar to theirs. All I do is find out what they are doing, then do the opposite!

The method-lead works on the Kennet as well.

Some venues are kind

CEMEX Angling Westhampnett

Steve 'Blobby' Larkcom had often talked of a venue on the outskirts of Chichester, one run at the time by RMC Angling, an organisation that he was actively involved with. The relatively untapped water for species other than carp, and the report of an accidental capture of an eel in excess of 8lb grasped my imagination, but gaining access to Westhampnett was impossible due to the fishing rights being leased out to a small syndicate, yet this was all about to change in the summer of 2005.

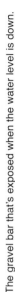

The gravel bar that's exposed when the water level is down.

RMC Angling had decided to add the venue to their portfolio and although the syndicate continued for a while, this was cut short for reasons unbeknown to me. This created a period of time between one syndicate ceasing and the other commencing, a period when the water needed protecting. It was decided that RMC bailiffs could fish the water during the close season, and it was during this time that Blobby and I were granted permission by Ian Welch to fish the venue, albeit for just one day.

Blobby had grown up in the surrounding area and fished Westhampnett many years before and after

picking him up, well before dawn, he described the venue in detail as we made our way through the back roads of Hampshire and West Sussex. It was still dark as he unlocked the gate at the Rutland end and after parking the car I remember hearing the odd carp crash in the stillness of the morning.

The previous winter and spring had been very dry and, as a result, the river Lavant that feeds the venue had failed to flow, leaving Westhampnett around five feet below its normal level. This revealed a long gravel bar that extended across the venue, cutting the lake into two which created a small, snag-ridden small lake to its left as well as leaving the main area of water to its right. Steve was adamant that we needed to be fishing off the main point, next to the refuse tip, so after driving the car along the bar and unloading the kit, we made our way around the margin.

This area is only accessible through the refuse tip entrance at the other end of the lake, yet this didn't open until 8am, and with no path, and still being dark, I remember struggling through brambles and stinging nettles to reach it. Sweating, bitten and stung, we eventually sat and watched the water as the sun rose. It soon became obvious that we were in the wrong area, as carp could be heard and seen crashing everywhere, but none in front of us, yet the moment wasn't wasted as I was to capture my first glimpse of the lake on film.

Steve fished, what I now know as peg 15, facing east toward the water sport complex, while I fished peg 17, facing west towards the Rutland end. Two hours passed without the slightest of indications so it was time to move. I could see carp moving in the small pond as well as jumping in the far corner, around the snags, so after fighting my way back to the car, decided to try to stalk a few.

Steve remained on the point while I assessed what I had in front of me. It was obvious that the day was going to turn into a scorcher and with carp already cruising just below the surface I knew that they would be up for a floater or two later on. Halfway along the gravel bar, I found a concrete pipe facing into the snaggy side and below this I spotted three good carp.

The water was crystal clear and watching these carp root around underneath the pipe was fascinating. Every now and again they would drift off, only to return a few minutes later to resume their feeding. Grabbing a bucket of hemp I waited for them to drift away before dropping a handful plus a couple of broken boilies below. Back they came and down went their heads, feeding with gay abandon before drifting off once more.

Stalked from under the concrete pipe.

This happened a couple more times, so, while gaining their confidence I had rigged up a barbel rod with 10lb line onto which a small pole float sat with a side-hooked boilie sitting below. The weight of the boilie sank the float and I had positioned this so that it sat just below the surface, as I knew when they returned line bites might just make me strike too early. What I wanted was for the float to rise out of the water and lie flat, indicating that a carp had sucked the bait in and lifted its head.

Watching through Polaroids, I vividly remember watching these three carp enter the swim, and then moments later the float lifting, me striking, and all hell being let loose. How I stopped this fish from reaching the sanctuary of the underwater tree stumps I don't know, but I did, and after a powerful fight slid the net under my first fish from Westhampnett, a mirror weighing 22lb 8oz, which was followed an hour later by a gorgeous 19lb 12oz mirror from the same spot.

Blobby had by now decided to give up the static style of fishing and was priming a few spots around the corner snags, only for a small bream to intercept his sweetcorn offering. By this time, I was up in the outlet

Westhampnett has some stunning carp as this 20 proves.

corner and once again found a group of carp, mainly small commons along with the odd bigger fish, and after firing out a few floaters managed to get these feeding. Singling out one of the bigger fish proved difficult and just when I though I had done this, a common of 12lb barged in. However, my persistence paid off with a dark chestnut-coloured mirror weighing 17lb.

I could see Blobby making his way down the road bank and looking somewhat stressed after being done on numerous occasions. While he was finding the carp extremely cute I was catching them with relative ease and watched as he headed up the refuse bank, where carp could be seen cruising. I headed to the north-east corner, an area which was very weedy and judging by the way the weed was lifting, there were a few lumps lurking below.

Half an hour passed before the first lips appeared and by the size of them I knew that in front of me was certainly a personal best carp. Blobby had also managed to get a few going on the surface and I watched as he struck into a big fish, only for his line to fall limp and his head to drop moments later.

Extremely dejected, Blobby walked round and settled next to me, describing what I had seen and confirming that it was a big fish he had lost. It was at this moment that I realised that I'd already had a fantastic day, and allowed Steve to have first cast at the fish that were now confidently feeding in front of me.

How a fish can turn a day, Steve with his floater caught 30.

Steve with the poached 20.

In places, it was like an aquarium.

It seemed to take an age for him to get his bait in the right position and I watched as he came agonisingly close, yet the angling god was watching, as moments later an explosion on the surface and a screaming clutch confirmed that his hook was firmly inside the mouth of the big lips I'd seen earlier.

The fight soon became slower as weed covered the fish, and as a huge lump slowly came ashore I jumped in and engulfed the lot with the net. Blobby's despair had changed to excitement and after clearing the weed, he found himself looking at a huge-framed carp which weighed 30lb 10oz. A couple of double-figure commons followed before the sun dropped, darkness fell, and two very happy anglers headed home.

Later that year, while enjoying a productive summer carp fishing on the River Thames, I repaid Ian Welch's generosity by taking him to one of my favourite spots on the river, and in the early hours his alarm sounded and his first-ever Thames carp graced his net, weighing 16lb 13oz.

It was a good move, as the following spring Ian once again allowed us to fish Westhampnett during the traditional close season and it only seemed right that my first visit should be with Blobby. Arriving with no key, we were forced to fish the double swim up from the outlet, yet we weren't complaining as lots of fish could be seen in this area. An angler had just vacated the swim after taking six carp, including two 30s and said that all his fish had come to his right-hand rod, so it was good to know that Blobby had remembered my generosity the previous spring and allowed me to choose sides.

My first off the top from Westi.

It was another blisteringly hot day and apart from a missed run early on, it seemed that we would have to go stalking once again. Before winding my rods in though, I needed to take a leak and so I strolled away from my rods for far longer than I should have. Returning a few minutes later, I found Matt, the head bailiff, in the swim and Blobby with a big mirror resting in his net.

I can't remember the sequence of events but after weighing her at 25lb 2oz and taking her pictures, I settled down hoping that one of my rods would burst into life. It was then that I noticed that my right-hand

rod indicator was hanging in the opposite direction to where I religiously position it. A few sarcastic remarks followed in the hope that Blobby would admit taking the fish on my rod but he stuck to his word that day, and for at least a couple of months afterwards, before giving in to my comments and admitting that he had taken it on my rod.

He had seen the head bailiff walking up the bank just after landing the fish, quickly wound both his rods in before launching mine back out, in the hope that I wouldn't question its capture, as well as not being caught with four rods out.

The snags in the west corner always held a few carp.

What a difference a fish makes!

It was while eel fishing that the lake's perch population was discovered. I had been fishing with Paul Garner all night for eels, using lobworm hookbaits. Paul had taken a number of eels throughout the night, with my rods strangely quiet, yet as dawn broke we were invaded by perch, the best weighing 2lb 15oz.

That spring also gave me a feel for the bream potential. I was standing watching a big 30lb mirror waddling past me, probably the Boilie Muncher, when I was drawn to a shoal of fish further out. As my eyes adapted to the surface glare, I gasped, as although bream weren't caught that often and their numbers unknown, here I was looking at hundreds, if not thousands, of very big bream, all grouped together, probably getting ready to spawn.

Here are the actual words taken from my diary written of one memorable session that spring:

Westhampnett, Monday May 15th 2005.

Arrived mid-afternoon and secured the Social swim which was good as although there was very little wind, what wind there was pushed directly into it. The clouds are dispersing as evening falls, yet the temperature remains in the mid-teens. In fact it feels muggy, perfect for eels. Fished two rods for eels and two for carp. The eel rods produced five eels to 3lb 13oz plus two perch

It's a capture that still comes up to this day, normally after we've had a few beers, and I mock him for his unscrupulous actions, yet we always end up laughing. After that incident you would have thought that the angling gods were watching, but come the end of the day, Blobby had managed another 20, this time an immaculate common of 23lb.

To be honest, Ian had allowed me on the lake, really to discover its eel potential, and although numerous came that spring, the biggest was just short of 4lb. It was while eel fishing that I decided two of my four rods would be rigged up for carp as they were always crashing out at distance. A snowman rig with a small PVA bag cast at showing fish soon proved its worth that spring, as numerous carp graced my net, including a personal best mirror of 31lb 6oz.

throughout the session with eels being caught during daylight! The carp rods fished with snowman rigs produced a personal best 31lb 6oz mirror at dusk to the distance rod plus three more at dawn, mirrors of 27lb 2oz, 18lb 15oz and a common of 13lb 8oz.

Matt, the head bailiff, was checking my permit when the 30 came; it's now obvious we're fishing for carp but I don't think he's that worried! Blobby fished the snags but amazingly received no action. This place is strange as when we fish together one of us usually has a result while the other struggles!

Once the venue became syndicated, I foolishly forgot to get my name on the list. I wasn't ever expecting to be able to fish the venue again, yet there was a twist of fate some years later that was to work in my favour.

A snowman rig cast at showing fish bought rewards with this mirror of 31lb 6oz.

233 - M

Spanish cats
The River Ebro

If there was one thing I wanted to see my dad catch, it was a catfish in excess of 100lb, and the most realistic chance of achieving this goal was to book a holiday on the River Ebro in Spain. Flying out of Heathrow, we arrived at Barcelona Airport where we were met by the guides from Catfish Capers and driven back to our base for the week, located in Capse, on the upper reaches of the river.

We didn't know what to expect, yet in less than an hour...

This was refined compared to what others were using!

The living accommodation, although not to be described as luxurious, was comfortable and over a curry that evening we met Martin Walker as well as everyone else who would be staying for the week. The guests were split into small parties; we were with a couple of young anglers from London. Each group received a guide who would look after our every need including cooking breakfast, packing lunches, driving to the venue, along with baiting up and landing fish. Everything seemed fairly organised and although we didn't fish that first day due to arriving quite late, we were soon receiving the early morning breakfast call the following day.

After a big English breakfast we were heading out of town and off-road along dusty narrow tracks, only known by the guides, sometimes followed by vultures that drifted menacingly on the thermals above. The river that year was very low and due to this we would have to negotiate steep banks when a run developed. It was also very warm, so plenty of fluids were needed as well as suntan lotion. Night fishing wasn't allowed in this area, which came as comforting news as I reckon the mosquitoes would have eaten us alive after dark.

The first day, we found ourselves fishing opposite a steep, mountainous outcrop, one with a deep glide directly below it. Winning the toss, Dad and I headed slightly downstream to an area where our bank was slightly more forgiving and comfortable, especially when it came to landing a fish. As soon as we picked up the rods we knew that these fish were going to be brutes, as we were to use 4lb test curve rods loaded with 100lb braid and 10oz leads to hold bottom, and this was in low water conditions!

Dad with his biggest-ever fish.

The rigs were simple running set-ups with big, sharp hooks and what can only be described as a horseshoe of extra-large pellets attached to them. The guide had returned from heading upstream to release the boat that had been secretly stashed away, and duly took our baits over to the far side of the river where they were dropped along with a few handfuls of very large halibut pellets. Rods were placed on rod pods with the tips high off the water and the baitrunner clicked on.

We really didn't know what to expect but in less than an hour we were to find out as one of the rods roared into life and I allowed Dad to grab it. I'm glad the clutches were set, as line ripped from a tight clutch and as Dad struggled to take the strain, I knew he would have been pulled into the water if it hadn't been. Eventually, the strain slowed the fish and the anxious look on Dad's face subsided. The guide had spotted Dad bent into the fish and was now knee-deep in mud waiting to hand the cat out for him. I'm not sure who was more surprised, Dad or me, as moments later he was struggling to lift his first-ever catfish, all 132lb of it!

A few minutes later, we watched as the guys from London played fish at the same time and I didn't have to wait too long either before my first Ebro catfish fell, although it was quite a bit smaller than Dad's at 69lb. The action continued throughout the day, often in small bursts, when one group would catch a few fish before seeing a lull, yet during such a lull the other party would be playing fish.

166lb of pellet-filled pussy.

It was as if the cats were moving up and down the river in groups. By the end of the first day, our arms were aching, we were covered in mud, but we had taken a further 11 cats, Dad taking fish of 116lb, 20lb, 83lb, 88lb and 96lb with me landing cats of 61lb, 58lb, 63lb, 98lb, 81lb and finally, one over the ton at 130lb!

Day two was spent in the same area and was almost a repeat performance of the first, with 12 cats being landed, Dad's best weighing 101lb, and mine, a whopping 138lb.

On days three and four, the swims were rotated, as this allowed the other anglers staying the week to enjoy a change of scenery, as well as fishing all the good swims. Unfortunately, we found ourselves off the fish on both days and could only muster up a further six fish to 90lb, while the lads from London enjoyed constant action taking a massive cat, and the best of the week at 166lb.

Something we had noticed during our stay was how many aborted runs we were getting and felt that the catfish weren't as stupid as some might think.

The upper reaches of the Ebro.

They just kept coming.

bored with this procedure and felt that there was absolutely no skill involved by allowing this to happen, so decided that on the final two days I would cast each rod out and bait up by catapult. The guide, to be frank, totally agreed with us, even mentioning that he would do the same if it were him, and even went to the trouble of showing how to glove a catfish out, the dangers involved in doing so, and then left us a glove to get on and fish properly.

Casting ten ounces of lead some 60 yards takes its toll, especially when I found myself working all four rods, but it seemed to work as the first three catfish were all over 100lb, the best 115lb. The action was noticeably slower that day and the guide told us that it was due to the easterly wind that had started to increase and the cold night we'd had previously.

The lads from London were catching a few, but were suffering from plenty of aborted takes, so noticing this, Dad and I positioned the rod tips upstream and instead of waiting for the alarms to scream, we watched. We were actually now quiver-tipping for cats. I had also removed the horseshoe-style bait band and simply tied two hairs off the hook, each containing two pellets, as I thought this might increase our catch rate. Looking back, I think it did, as we continued to catch over the duration of our stay, adding another ten cats to our tally.

The cats get fished for most days, see the same tactics day in day out, and we felt that many of the dropped runs were from fish simply feeling the resistance and spitting the bait out. We also felt that it was so easy to let the guide row the hookbaits out, drop the rigs and half a sack of pellets on top, only for us to sit back and wait. Although I was thankful for the guides' help in achieving our goal, I soon became

Our total for the week was 44 cats, including 11 over 100lb, but although the experience was one I will always remember, totally enjoyed, and would highly recommend, I was slightly disappointed with the variety of the fishing as no big carp showed.

Taking the strain.

A happy man.

My biggest of the holiday.

Silver bream British record

Mill Farm Fishery

It was in the spring of 2003 that Mill Farm Fishery started to get my attention. Dennis Flack's silver bream record that had stood for many years at 15oz had finally been broken, not once but twice, firstly by a fish of 1lb 4oz and then with another of 1lb 11oz.

Target reached; a British record.

Plans were made, and early one morning in May my father and I found ourselves heading south, through the scenic county of West Sussex with silver bream on our minds, a species nether of us had caught before.

Neither of us knew what to expect but some research had shown us that it was the middle lake, Mill, that had been producing the record-breakers and it was here that we settled early that morning. I had made an earlier recce session after reading about the venue in Angler's Mail, but on arrival found the lake closed until Easter, but this had at least sorted out the route and how long it took.

Having absolutely no idea how silver bream feed and what other species the lake held, we loose-fed maggots and fished the pole. However, it soon became apparent that this approach only attracted the huge amounts of carp, and time after time we found ourselves having to tie new hooklinks after being smashed up. The odd silver did appear but this was only when the bait found the bottom and it was this that had my brain working overtime on how to target this species on future trips. I estimated our total weight of fish caught that first trip exceeded 130lb, made up of carp, crucians, tench, roach, eels and small silvers and remember connecting with a fish just before packing up that felt slightly different.

After years of fishing, you can make an educated guess on what fish you have hooked and 95 per cent of the time you are right, but here I was connected to something that angrily shook its head before gliding outwards and upwards. As it hit surface, I saw it was a big silver and took things carefully, soon finding out that silver bream aren't like bronze bream, and fight right to the end. In the net I knew that I had achieved my target set at one pound and on the scales she went 1lb 4oz.

We visited the lake a few more times that season but although no bigger silver bream came, I did find a solution to avoiding the carp and that came in the form of a bait dropper. It was a tactic that was to serve me well, yet although we visited the venue the following year the biggest silver only weighed 1lb 6oz. However, I felt that it was only a matter of time before something special turned up, as by now my catch was being dominated by silvers.

A couple of visits soon after Easter in 2005 saw our catch rate of silvers increasing. In the past I was catching around a 100lb of fish on each visit by loose-feeding maggots, but couldn't be selective. Now though, after perfecting the use of a bait dropper and altering my shotting pattern, very few nuisance fish were being caught, and I was going home contented with 30lb of silvers. As for Dad, he's happy just catching and continued to loose-feed, catching far more than me on most occasions, and deep down I knew that for him it was a numbers game, but if a big silver entered my swim, then there was a very good chance I would connect with it.

Witnesses and weighing.

Below are the words taken from my diary of a very special day:

Mill Farm Fishery, Thursday 14th April 2005.

My sixth sense did not disappoint me, as the night before leaving was a restless one, and I had a gut feeling that something special was about to happen. Arriving at opening time, on an overcast, cold day, things did not look good and with the bait dropper tactic not working as well as usual, we felt that it was not going to be our day. Bites were few and far between, probably due to a cold easterly wind, and we really had to work for them, but small groups of fish kept us interested.

At 11am, unbeknown to me, a big silver had entered my swim and was soon to find my worm and maggot cocktail. As soon as she was hooked, I knew it was something special and after a brief fight she dropped over the drawstring before being weighed. At 1lb 13oz 8drams she recorded a new British record, something deep down I

Kevin matches my British record.

Dad enjoyed the non-stop action.

was aware was about to happen. The day wasn't over and an hour later I caught another big silver bream, this time weighing 1lb 6oz, a brace I won't forget in a hurry. The day ended at 4pm, with a dozen other silvers, the odd roach and a dozen crucians, one species that was difficult to avoid. Dad had a similar catch but with far fewer silvers and more carp.

We visited the lake on a number of occasions soon after, but once the silver bream had spawned, thoughts were that my record was safe, yet on June 15th Kevin joined me and went on to catch another big silver weighing exactly the same as my record-breaker,

proof that the fish I had caught wasn't the biggest in the lake at the time.

It's a long story why it took so long to ratify my silver bream by the BRFC as a record, but in short, it seemed to take forever initially for them to identify the fish. I then received the master copies of my claim forms back in the post, something that absolutely amazed me, as they asked if I could send these to my first witness for signing, and then, when and if I received them back, send them to the second. It was a risky process; one I wasn't happy proceeding with, so I took photocopies of the originals.

These were sent back to the BRFC, with the copies being sent to each witness, along with stamped addressed envelopes addressed to the BRFC. All I could now do was sit back with my fingers crossed. Months passed, during which time a bigger silver bream was caught, again from Mill Farm Fishery, and with the angler making a claim, when my certificate was finally issued, it once again was classified as an interim British record. Ten guesses where I display this!

Mill Farm Fishery was a venue that we continued to visit over the next few years. It's set in wonderful scenery with the rolling hills of the South Downs as a backdrop. Even on a bad day you can catch plenty of fish, however it wasn't until 2009 that I almost regained my title.

The venue's bailiff, Adrian, had always mentioned that the biggest silver bream lived in the Specimen Lake. We had been content fishing Mill Lake, but it was obvious that trying to beat the 2lb barrier from here was unlikely. We headed for the Specimen Lake and I initially tried float fishing for the silvers, but it's far shallower and I had limited success. Reassessing the situation, I finally opted for a completely contrasting tactic, the helicopter rig, but only after seeing its effectiveness on catching big silvers demonstrated by Mick Martin who had joined me for a day in attempt to catch his first-ever of the species.

Clipped up and casting to a small island, I watched as he played, landed, and then waved to me for some assistance. In his net was a massive silver bream, far bigger than I had ever seen and on the scales she pulled the needle round to 2lb 3oz, but once again, there was no point making a claim as a slightly bigger fish was going through the claim procedure.

Mick Martin took the first-ever brace of two-pounders.

The Specimen Lake are where the big ones lived.

Caught on the same day as the record.

patches of bubbles could be seen; fish were definitely feeding, but were they silver bream? Using worm and maggot cocktails I cast both rods close to the island margin, and was relieved to see the indicators settle, as on occasions small roach can make this approach almost impossible. After a number of tench I found myself attached to a fish that felt altogether different and thoughts of a big silver were soon proved right when one fell into the net.

It was obvious that this fish was close to, if not bigger than the British record and on the scales she went 2lb 9oz, later that day to be joined with another slightly bigger at 2lb 9oz 8drams. That week, the actual weight of the biggest silver bream to be taken from the venue became somewhat confusing. In fact, I think the record fell three times during that period. Thoughts were that Doug Plant had secured a place in the history books with a silver of 2lb 11oz, yet unbeknown to me, on the far bank, on the same day as my big brace, an angler had landed an even bigger specimen, this time weighing 2lb 14oz.

It was a capture that became even more notable as later in the day Mick hooked and landed another silver, this time weighing exactly 2lb and he was the first angler ever to record such a remarkable brace.

Being beaten by the girlfriend's dad came with plenty of teasing, something that made me even more determined, but I was only subjected to this for a couple of weeks as my next session saw a 2lb 1oz specimen being landed. This still wasn't quite good enough for me; however, the next session changed all this.

It was a perfect morning for fishing, overcast, still and mild and listening to a Cuckoo in the surrounding hills only heightened my expectancy, as spring had arrived. Looking across the lake, small

Every year, news filters through the grapevine of silver bream in excess of 3lb coming from the venue. I'm sure one day the British best will exceed this, however targeting a British record is far harder now than back in the early days, as the lakes have seen an influx of tiny silvers. Using maggot and worm isn't an option anymore and when the record falls, I would be surprised if it comes on such a bait. With the carpers attaching PVA bags full of high-protein pellets next to their bigger hookbaits, it's impossible to predict just how big the silver bream will grow, yet what I did predict was that it would probably be an angler who scaled down a similar approach who would succeed in breaking the 3lb barrier.

In May 2012, news came through that the silver bream record had fallen again. I wasn't surprised to hear that the 3lb barrier had been broken, it was only a matter of time, and as I predicted, it had been taken by an angler scaling down and using pellet.

Well done to Gareth Evans, with a magnificent silver weighing 3lb 5oz!

They just keep getting bigger.

Roach captures - The last few years

The Pallatrax Winner

One of the many magazines to disappear over the last few years was 'Southern Angler', but while it was running, its Pallatrax Yearly Competition drew a highly competitive following.

Brace from River Farm Fishery.

I managed to qualify for the final, held at Pallington Specimen Lake near Dorchester, for two years running, after entering a number of specimen fish, and to be honest, this competition took priority over all others. Held during the first week of September, contestants would compete to catch a list of different species, and each one would have points awarded, dependant on their size.

The first year, Dad also qualified after capturing a brace of huge barbel from the river Loddon and as we travelled down together he joked about sharing the £1000 winnings. Drawn on different sides to the lake, the call came in that after just an hour Dad had caught a roach weighing 2lb 1oz, a capture rich in points. Hours passed, and as the fishing toughened up, I began to think that there might just be a chance that Dad could take the title, yet with some of the best specialist anglers surrounding the lake, I tried not to get over-excited.

I had fished all night, taking numerous fish, but none over the qualifying mark, and with just an hour to go, and after having had no sleep, decided to cast out bright yellow pop-ups toward the island and grab some shut-eye. Ten minutes before the whistle blew, I remember getting a one-toner and grabbing the rod, but after sleeping on my left arm I was unable to grab the handle and wind in as my arm was dead. Numerous people watched, unaware of my situation and after a few seconds, the fish reached the sanctuary of the island and shed the hook.

Looking back, Dad's roach had rewarded him with 20 points, and a 20lb carp was also worth 20 points, so to lose, what felt like a very big carp in the dying minutes was actually a blessing in disguise, as come the end of the match, Dad won with his roach, left with complete honours, and I found myself holding a cheque for £500!

The following year was a closer contest, with all anglers catching, and one that could have seen anyone winning. Once again, the weather did its best to dampen our spirits, however, after catching most species and staying awake for 24 hours, the trophy was awarded to an elderly gentleman, whose name escapes me. Contestants were allocated a few hours throughout the 24-hour match to fish for dace and grayling on the River Frome, and it was a specimen grayling that clinched the title.

The one I lost was far bigger.

Littleton North, home of some massive roach, but could I find them?

CEMEX Angling Littleton North, K1 and River Farm Fishery in Titchfield, 2009 – 2011.

Although in a specialist world roach have always been respected as one of the most sought-after fish, especially river roach, the time I have allocated to catch one of specimen proportions, apart from when I fished Willow Pool in Oxfordshire and the River Itchen in Hampshire, has been somewhat limited.

Yet, saying this, I have always found myself following up leads regarding the species, and this has lead me to many a water. CEMEX Angling K1 and Littleton North are two that are worthy of a mention, as both have the potential to produce very big roach.

Littleton North was a venue that I spent a number of nights on, and although I enjoyed every minute spent there, I found it very difficult to target roach, due to the amount of small eels. My main line of attack was the helicopter rig baited with maggots fished over hemp, but the tactic was almost impossible to use, even in the winter, and although roach exceeding 2lb exist, conventional tactics seem ineffective, and I'm not surprised that most specimen roach are caught by accident, usually by carp anglers using boilies.

Day-ticket roach fishing doesn't get much better.

CEMEX Angling Kingsmead is a venue with huge potential. It's deep, weedy, and has everything I feel is needed to produce a massive roach, yet very few anglers have fished for them. I spent a couple of nights fishing the swims in the Kennel car park, and on my very first night, using heli-rigs and maggots, took a roach weighing 2lb 1oz, along with losing one much bigger at the net.

The few nights spent after this were interrupted by eels, the best weighing 4lb 10oz, but it was an exceptionally mild start to the winter, and for roach fishing, I believe it needs to be really cold. I'd love to have the time to explore this venue in more depth, but unfortunately, I don't think it will ever happen.

River Farm Fishery, located near Titchfield in Hampshire, must have been one of the best kept secrets in angling. For years, I watched as 2lb-plus roach were reported, but could I locate the venue? No! That was until a reporter for the Angler's Mail accidentally mentioned the big roach that were being caught on a carp venue he was fishing.

It was ironic that at the very same time, my father, through endless hours of research, had come to the same conclusion and located the water for himself after overhearing a discussion in his local tackle shop. Unfortunately, every other roach angler in the country had come to the same conclusion and for the best part

My best from River Farm weighed 2lb 6oz.

of two years getting a swim on the tiny former trout pond was never a certainty. The fishing, though, during those first few years was simply amazing, and catching a 2lb roach on most occasions, was almost guaranteed. The additional benefit was the huge head of immaculate common carp that often interrupted the roach sessions; they were always a welcome bonus.

The biggest roach that I landed from the venue is 2lb 6oz, a fish that was full of spawn, so although a two-pounder wasn't difficult, most caught were just scrapers by an ounce or so. A variety of methods work, from fishing the waggler over sprayed maggot, to using a delicate pole float in the margins, yet by far the most devastating rig was the helicopter rig, simply cast to the centre of the lake.

Unfortunately, over the last few years there has been an explosion of small roach. These are normally removed every two years, which gives the carp and bigger roach plenty of space; just what they need to grow big. For some reason, this two-year netting operation was missed and unless it's reinstated, I fear that the fishery will go from being one of the best roach waters in the country, to simply a mediocre day-ticket venue.

We went home £1000 richer.

Immaculate two-pounder.

Are we guesting? Yep!

River Itchen

A 2lb river roach is rare, so when news filtered through the grapevine of numbers being taken from a free stretch of the River Itchen, close to Winchester, I had to investigate. Blobby was informative and keen to capitalise on this information so we made plans to make an exploratory session to try to locate them.

It was the winter of 2006, a time when we were both enjoying some fabulous grayling fishing further downstream around Eastleigh, so to pull away from there and to start searching somewhere completely new was difficult. However, after some rain, and the thought of a coloured river, we headed to Winnall, full of expectancy.

Blobby's informant had mentioned that the area where the roach were located was in a so-called 'grey area', a section of river that might well be a no-fishing area, but on our arrival, we couldn't see any 'no fishing' signs, just notices informing the public that dogs should be kept on leads and that cycling was prohibited. This was good enough for us, and we took the attitude that until we were told otherwise, we would commence fishing, albeit in a stealthy manner.

Our first trip was in early January 2006, and although that trip proved fruitless, we noticed areas of the bank that showed signs of fishing. Numerous short trips were made after this, most coinciding with the best parts of the day, dawn and dusk; however, it was while trotting through a swim further downstream, behind an industrial estate, that I hit the jackpot.

While manoeuvring a float through what we called 'the jungle', I spotted what looked like a fish roll further downstream. Blobby had resigned himself to the big bend upstream and was confident that the big roach were there, yet unbeknown to him, I had made a chance encounter, one that I was about to capitalise on.

Moving downstream and positioning myself above a long run, I deposited a small handful of mashed bread in the swim before dropping a pinch of flake offered under a loafer style float. Ten yards downstream, the float dipped, then buried, and I found myself bent into a sizeable fish. A few moments later I slid the net under a big roach, not quite 2lb, but a fish that was to be the beginning of a period in time that won't be forgotten. I rested the roach in the net, the next cast met with a similar result and by the time the light had faded a dozen or more, pound-plus roach sat in the folds of my net. Blobby had taken a few smaller roach and grayling from upstream, and at last we felt we had discovered what can only be described as a little gem.

For the following two winters we visited the stretch, normally when we felt the river was slightly 'out of sorts' for grayling and over that period we enjoyed consistent and reliable sport, yet one thing was missing, more than one 2lb roach. Our informant had told us that his student had been catching numerous 2lb plus roach, including one with a broken back, weighing over three, yet, after numerous recaptures, the best I took was 2lb 4oz.

It was still a fantastic fish, and to this day a river best for me, but miles short of what we had been led to believe. On most occasions, whoever fished opposite the car park, seemed to catch around a dozen roach, yet, although many weighed an ounce or two short of the magical 2lb barrier, only one surpassed this, and this one of 2lb 4oz was a strange shape, some might say looking as if it had a broken back!

Unfortunately, the shoal became otter food.

A moody night on the river.

It was soon agreed that we had pretty much discovered the roach stock within the stretch and settled that the reports of numerous 2lb roach and one over three were wildly exaggerated, yet catching roach well over the pound was rare and we often frequented the stretch whenever a few hours allowed.

On one occasion, I had to witness the sickening sight of seeing a muscovy duck floating downstream in a dazed state, as two suspicious characters followed it. Trying to protect the duck and prevent it from drifting under the bridge and into the weir, as well as away from the dodgy-looking characters, I finally phoned the Hampshire and Isle of Wight Trust, the governing body that controlled the stretch, yet with limited resources it seemed pointless and no one came. However, as darkness fell, the bird seemed to regain consciousness and I left, feeling I had done my best.

I'm fairly sure that the bird survived and, at the time, all thoughts of catching roach were quickly dismissed, but that call probably did us no good, as while fishing the following week, at first light, we were approached by a warden who politely told us that fishing in this area wasn't allowed.

Fair play, we'd had our fill and were ready to move on, but I just wonder, by allowing certain anglers access to such areas, would this help in its protection? In my eyes, yes, but since that last visit I have been informed that otters are now on the beat and so catching a specimen roach has been lost forever. Sign of the times, I'm afraid.

2lb 4oz warrior from the Itchen.

Brief
encounters

Lynch Hill's, Willow Pool

Willow Pool on the Lynch Hill Complex in Oxfordshire, often referred to as a southern stillwater, has to be the best roach venue in the country, not just for the sheer numbers of huge roach that thrive in this deep, clear venue, but for its sheer consistency over so many years.

I recall reading numerous articles by specimen anglers on this water and wondered whether the time would ever come, when I would be fortunate enough to walk the path to this special place. This opportunity finally came while I was working as a tackle consultant for Wychwood and while talking to Paul Garner, we decided to team up, and tackle this venue. Paul had fished the water a number of years before and I felt honoured that such a fantastic angler wanted my company, and with his knowledge, felt that I was halfway to the fish of a lifetime, a 3lb roach.

Unfortunately, work commitments caught up with Paul and as a result I was left alone, feeling completely out of my depth, as never before had I fished such a deep venue for one of our most difficult of all species, and certainly not throughout the winter.

On the back foot from the start, I remember one evening spending hours flicking through numerous copies of Coarse Angling Today in search of articles explaining the helicopter rig and the venue. Slowly, my knowledge grew, and when November arrived, rods and tackle had

Med 1 was the most prolific, if you could get in there!

been prepared for my first session. Plans had been made to spend as much time on the venue as I could, as the cost of the ticket was a big outlay at the time, and I needed to justify this with results.

My first session came early in November, even after being told to forget the venue until December, as an explosion of small perch was making presenting maggot hookbaits a real nightmare. However, eager to familiarise myself with the place, I still travelled up during the first week of the month.

Setting up in what I now know as Med 2, I cast out the standard two-hook helicopter rigs until I felt the feeders hit clear spots with a solid thud. Clipping the line in the reel's line clip and placing a stop knot made of pole elastic just off the rod top, I made a dozen casts to the same spot before attaching the lightweight bobbins and sitting back. It only took seconds for the indicator to dance, and the first of many nuisance perch intercepted the bait. Unfortunately, these didn't slow down after dark and I found myself changing the maggot hookbait to corn, only to lose a very big carp in the early hours. I'd made my acquaintance with the famous Willow Pool, yet it wasn't one I care to remember.

A couple of weeks later, I found myself back once again, this time in what was later to be regarded as the flyer, Med 1.

Although I had helicopter rigs with me, I felt that a better approach, and a more conventional tactic, was to fish a small maggot feeder on a running line in conjunction with a quivertip. Set up match style, I remember Alan Storey, one of Willow's greatest anglers, stopping for a chat and recall his words, "It's nice to see someone giving the roach some respect."

Mike picked up my rod while I was taking a leak.

It was this compliment and his encouraging words that saw me determined to catch a big roach on such tactics, and although that day I took numerous roach, the biggest was around a pound, along with the occasional better perch.

I packed up well after dark, and I remember bumping into someone who I classify as one of the best specimen anglers of our generation, Adrian Smith. He had timed his arrival to avoid the traffic, one that would allow him to pick a swim ready for the morning. I'm sure Adrian dropped his tackle in the swim I had just vacated, yet just beginning to understanding what makes a brilliant angler, I'm sure he never took this finding for granted, and spent hours picking a swim using what my dad had taught me - watercraft.

Catching on the tip felt so much better.

It was late in November when my dream came true. Arriving late one afternoon, I stopped to talk to regular, Mike Townsend, who was set up in Med 1. I owe him for pointing me into the Hump swim at the bottom of the right-hand bank, and now smile, as I recall him mentioning that he was torn between the two, and that by 'sod's law' I would catch a 3lb roach later that evening.

Three hours later, and just into darkness, I vividly remember watching the isotope on my quivertip tap before pulling round, and as I had set out to do, not only landed the fish dreams are made of, but took it on my preferred method. My first proper roach from the venue weighed exactly 3lb and, unfortunately for Mike, he was on the wrong side of the lens, yet strangely, I knew that the angling gods would repay him, and over the next few seasons, they did just that. It wasn't the only specimen I took that night, as once my eyes started playing games with the isotope, heli-rigs were cast out and roach of 2lb 5oz and 2lb 10oz graced my net.

I'm not sure why my love for the venue dwindled after these captures, maybe it was because a challenge that I had expected to take for so long, came to fruition so quickly, but for some reason I couldn't settle and never felt 100 per cent comfortable again. Don't get me wrong, the venue is fascinating, and its inhabitants mind-blowing, I just think I was a victim of circumstance, and for reasons I don't want to comment on, only fished the lake half a dozen more times before calling it a day.

During those final few outings, I did manage to land a few more specimen roach, all on helicopter rigs, but I never felt completely competent using them and lost far more than I caught due to hooklink breakages, hook-pulls or aborted runs. It was certainly a learning curve and I do believe that it was this venue that channelled me into the thinking and methodical angler I am today. So, although I have mixed emotions on such a prolific and amazing water, I do feel that I owe it, for conditioning myself into the way I think today and I don't regret one second spent mesmerised by its ambience.

The following year, I was fortunate to be invited back by my good friend, Mike Townsend. We had tried to organise a three-day trip in December but on the morning in question I awoke to six inches of snow. Still optimistic and eager, I loaded the car, only to close the boot and end up like a giant snowman! With wheels spinning out of the drive and after just a few miles down the road, common sense took over, and I made the call to Mike who by this time was heading south from his Doncaster home and was in the grip of a snowstorm. The trip was abandoned, but come January we were back, and along with Dai Gribble set up not quite knowing what was in store. The lake was busy and the fishing was slow, yet on such a venue, you only need one bite, and that knowledge drives us specimen anglers to go to such measures in our quest to succeed.

As darkness fell on the first evening, my indicators danced twice. I was watching them on both occasions and both were from two-pound roach, but it was the third bite on the following morning, that produced the biggest, yet it wasn't me that landed the fish, as I was relieving myself in the bushes behind when the bite developed.

The witching hour.

Mike was standing next to my rods and from a distance I shouted to him to pick the rod up, which turned out to be the biggest fish of the trip, weighing 2lb 10oz.

The following night, a storm blew up and I decided to abandon the oval and erect a bivvy, very uncharacteristic of me, and I recall Dai walking by and asking if I had planning permission for such a monstrosity.

On the last night, Dai managed a modest fish and I took another two, yet it was Mike who left the happier man, as he had received no bites during his stay, but was leaving having landed the biggest fish of the weekend. It was during this session that Mike mentioned that rudd had started to show in their catches. At the time, I thought he was going slightly doolally due to his lack of action, as rudd don't feed in winter, they're summer fish.

A week later, another good friend, Adrian Eves, called to say that he had just taken a 2lb rudd from Frensham Great Pond on a lobworm intended for perch. The following week I found myself on Frensham, casting out helicopter rigs and come the end of the night, I had landed an insane amount of tench, as well as a 2lb rudd!

To many, Willow may seem easy, a place that only a few are privileged to fish, yet it's open to all, you just need to put your name on the waiting list and wait, like everyone else has done. All we ever read in the

weekly magazines is when an angler has a big hit, a time when he gets his tactics correct and falls on the fish that have shoaled tightly, soon to spawn, yet Willow is far from easy. I was the top rod on the weekend which saw four fish fall in 72 hours, many others blanked, or took just one fish, so if you think it's easy, then think again, it's a real head-banger!

The target three came too quickly.

Paradise lost
CEMEX Angling Frimley Complex

When Frimley is mentioned, most think of Pit 3, home of some of England's biggest and best-looking common carp, yet as an all-round specimen angler, it wasn't these that interested me, but the small stock of massive bream that lived within it. I was also interested in Pit 4, The Donut, and it was this lake that I first walked round. However, after doing the circuit, it left me with little to go on, and apart from one small featureless island, the crystal clear, weedy water did little to inspire me.

Steve thought I had two tench sacked up!

couple of anglers fishing the lake and made a quick phone call to Donut knowing jolly well he was going to jump at the chance of fishing such an historic venue if I offered it to him.

After organising the required passes, we planned a two-night session the following week, and with a feature pencilled in with 'Coarse Fisherman' on bream fishing, tactics had to be modified so we would stand a chance of catching a few.

Starting off in a couple of swims at the railways end, Donut used 14mm Richworth Tutti Frutti boilies fished alongside method feeders and was fortunate to catch a stunning old mirror weighing 28lb, on the first night. I used a catapult to deposit a big bed of groundbait into open water that was laced with dead maggots and corn, and proceeded to blank.

The following morning, I awoke and saw that the wind had swung and was pushing hard up toward the island, and finally managed to persuade Donut to move. The same tactics were employed and apart from losing a big carp on the maggots, I blanked once again.

Crossing the path I entered the gate to Pit 3 and straight away saw that this lake oozed features, and after watching numerous large common carp drift unconcernedly between the newly sprouting lilies, felt instantly attracted to its beauty. Expecting to see most swims taken, I was pleasantly surprised to find just a

I'm not sure if anyone can relate to this, but all I remember was that I awoke to a one-toner and although I remember playing the fish, at the time I had absolutely no idea where I was, or even if I was fishing in this country. I must have been half-asleep, probably due to Donut who had woken me on numerous occasions throughout the night, first with a 22lb 5oz common, followed by another of 32lb 15oz, followed by a 12lb 11oz bream and just to rub it in, finished with a 6lb 13oz tench. The article was called 'Every Dog Has Its Day' and by the end, all I could do was throw in the towel and admit to being well and truly stuffed.

We fished the venue a couple of times after this, but without any joy, and I started to paint a picture that the venue didn't hold as many bream as I had been lead to believe. However, the ones that were still in the venue were big, and the chance of a 16-plus bream was possible.

It was while fishing this lake that I stumbled on Pit 2. No more than a couple of acres and surrounded by trees, this little water looked like it had been lost in time. I asked a few of the bailiffs about the stock and they replied that it had some stunning carp up to 30lb, along with a very good head of tench, plus a few bream and crucians.

The more I looked at the lake, the more I felt myself drawn to it. The lake saw very little angling pressure and as night fishing was only allowed to bailiffs or Gold Card holders, I persuaded CEMEX Angling to grant me a few passes in return for the possibility of the odd article.

The commons were stunning.

A few days later, and having some time on my hands, I decided to take a slow walk around the lake and the peg that I was instantly drawn to was number seven, or should I say lucky peg seven. It had three main features in the form of an overhanging tree to its left, with a deep, sloping gravel margin dropping off underneath, as well as the main island positioned also to the left, along with open water to the right. Three rods were allowed so it seemed the obvious starting point.

I was back a couple of days later armed with a few pints of red maggots, hemp and some corn just in case the maggots proved unsuccessful. I decided to fish helicopter rigs baited with double red maggot on two of my rods, one alongside the island, the other in open water and having a few hours to spare before darkness fell, I decided to set up a float rod and fish alongside the overhanging tree.

An hour had passed and after a few suspicious bubbles started to pop up around the float, I found myself playing a deep, heavy fish. I was only using a 3lb hooklink and a tiny size 18 hook, so when the biggest tench I'd ever seen came swimming past, in

As it waddled past, I just had to drop the net under it.

a way that it seemed not to know it was hooked, I stretched out the landing net and scooped up my prize. I couldn't quite believe what I was looking at, as this tench had shoulders like a carp and on the scales swung the needle round to 10lb 3oz, setting a new personal best. Five more tench followed, all on the maggot and helicopter rigs and they were all good fish in the 5 to 7lb bracket. I had found paradise and before leaving, spodded out the remaining dead maggots and hemp with a view to returning two days later. I just hoped that the swim would be free.

Back at the lake, a horrid, cold, easterly wind had sprung up, the swim was free though, yet my confidence wasn't high for catching. However, I was surprised when the odd tench rolled late in the afternoon and when the indicator sprang into life, I once again found myself dropping the net under a big tench, this time weighing 7lb 13oz. No more action came that evening and when darkness fell, the tench stopped showing, but I was tempted to fish later than allowed, as I was getting quite a few liners.

Donut took this big bream from Pit 3.

The following week, I had arranged a tench feature with Angling Times and planned to fish the night before to get the swim going and I hoped to sack a couple of good tench (permission had been granted for the use of sacks for this feature). That night, I found out just what the liners were caused by, and after catching a couple of 6lb tench in the evening, I settled down expecting the night to be hectic.

Just like the previous week, as darkness fell the tench stopped rolling and the liners started, yet it was a couple of hours later that the indicator dropped to the ground and I found myself playing a fish that although it felt heavy, did little apart from shake its head.

As I shone the head torch out into the mist-covered lake, a great big bream surfaced before being swallowed up in the landing net.

First impression was that I had beaten Donut's best from Pit 3, but although it was a new personal best, it dropped a few ounces short. The bream was safely sacked and it wasn't long before a repeat performance saw a second of similar size filling the other sack. The liners then stopped and the lake came alive with carp jumping everywhere. The events of that evening and night, as well as the morning were similar to most, it was as if every species had a routine, and just before first light the alarm screamed and a 20lb common graced the bank.

Steve Partner was on his way and I remember the mobile ringing shortly after returning the carp. He was eager to know what I had caught, and I told him that I had a couple of doubles sacked up, but forgot to tell him what species these were. As we had arranged a tench feature, I chuckled as I sat back and imaged Steve smiling like a Cheshire cat with his foot hard on the accelerator, trying to beat the morning traffic.

Tench fishing at its best.

As you can imagine, those first few sessions saw me falling in love with the venue and I spent numerous memorable nights after this, gripped in its atmosphere along with experiencing some of the best tench fishing I've ever had. Although I never came close to beating that first tench, many were well over 7lb and the 20lb carp and double-figure bream created fantastic diversity.

I never caught a big crucian from the venue but there was one night when many an oily swirl was noticed right under my rod tips, almost certainly made by these. I did fish a couple of nights in search of crucians, using scaled-down bolt-rigs and single pieces of corn fished right in the margins, but all I caught were double-figure bream!

Unfortunately, this little piece of paradise was lost, as during the severe winter of 2010 and after being frozen for a lengthy period, it suffered from an oxygen deficiency which killed most, if not all of its stock. Although it was only carp that were reported in the press, I fear that all the other species fell victim too, and a venue that I could have easily spent the rest of my life on was lost forever.

Everything I caught was huge.

My second home

Frensham Great Pond

As I peeled the chest waders off and sat on the side of the bed chair looking across the water, my thoughts were, 'What the hell am I doing here?' A bed of hemp and maggots had been spodded out to a spot at 60 yards and two helicopter rigs cast so they fell upon it, one baited with two red maggots spiced up with turmeric, the other again with two red maggots, only these had been popped-up on the three-inch hooklink by adding a sliver of rig foam, maggot-shaped.

It was the 23rd of February 2009 and the view looked bleak. Anyone who knows Frensham Great Pond will know it's not the most welcoming of venues in the winter, as its 60 or more windswept acres and sand-covered ground absorbs the cold making it feel raw. What's worse is that its shallow nature and tree-lined margins mean that you have to wade out in most swims to cast, something only the bravest will do to catch a fish.

Darkness was falling and I started to question my sanity, blaming Mike Townsend and Adrian Eves for finding myself in this position, then suddenly, one of the alarms sounded. Just one bleep, and I thought, 'no it can't be,' but as the indicator dropped then pulled up tight I thought, 'oh yes it is.' Lifting the rod and feeling into the fish, I watched as the rod took on a satisfying curve before line started to leave the spool. This was no rudd, my intended quarry, but a tench, one of nine to grace my net that night, along with a 2lb 4oz perch but it was the rudd that shocked me, three in fact, the biggest 2lb 5oz!

From that day on, I have never looked back and although I cursed my mates under my breath that very first evening, I have to apologise and thank them kindly, as if it were not for them, we would all still be thinking that rudd only get caught in the summer.

I couldn't wait to get back. Was this just a fluke? Maybe, as just one tench came on the next session. However, teaming up with Donut a few days later saw us land numerous tench and rudd, both recording a brace of twos. Having stumbled on such an eye-opening experience and with time running out before the traditional close season closed the water, I crammed in as many nights as I could, seven in fact, in just 12 days.

Here are the actual words taken from my diary of one of these sessions:
Frensham Great Pond, Wednesday 9th March 2009.

Conditions: Perfect, with a gentle south-westerly, overcast and mild at seven degrees.
Duration of session: Overnight.
Tactics: First three hours of darkness on the float then feeders thereafter.
Result: 11 tench plus around 40 rudd, including seven two-pounders. Three came on the float, the best 2lb 11oz 8drams and four on the feeders, the best 2lb 14oz!

One night I called Donut insane as he waded out into the darkness with a starlight attached to a waggler. Sitting back, I watched as he sprayed maggots and then cast, and thought, 'he will never catch', only moments later to be bent into a rudd. Three hours was the maximum length of time we were able to stand in the water before all feeling was lost in our legs and I remember one night when a snowstorm blew across the lake. We were both float fishing and catching big rudd, laughing like kids, saying 'this should never happen!' It was a really remarkable, historic period, a spell when no fewer than 19, 2lb rudd graced my net, including one three-pounder which happened to be the last rudd that year. Numerous smaller rudd were also caught, along with a number of perch, as well as a staggering 80 tench.

I never get bored with Frensham's beauty.

The waggler fishing can be spectacular in the summer.

Although Frensham can look bleak and feel raw in the depths of winter, it sure makes up for this in the summer. The countryside surrounding the lake is just breathtaking with sloping hills covered in purple heather which create a habitat that supports an immense variety of plants and animals, some of which are nationally very rare. The reed-fringed margins house an abundance of natural food, which does create a few problems, as the tench and rudd seem to have an endless supply of food come late July, August and September, a period that can be extremely frustrating for the angler. The lake also suffers from huge, blue-green algae blooms that again make the water look unwelcoming and a word of warning to any bathers, watch out for water fleas. I found out the hard way once while collecting water snails for bait in shorts and ended up with over 70 incredibly itchy bites on my legs.

The first six weeks of the season is without doubt the best time to fish and there's no better way than to stand out in the lake and fish a float. Mornings are certainly best for the tench, until around 10am. A lull then commences, just like most lakes before the rudd move in, usually an hour before dusk, feeding hard until midnight when they disappear.

There's no better way of catching them in the summer than on the float.

Who would have thought - rudd in winter?

Although the helicopter rig works in the winter, I consider it as the lazy option in the summer, anyone using it is really missing out, and I can't think of anything better than watching the tip of a float among a mass of bubbles gently lift then slide away. Float fishing at Frensham really is fishing at its best.

As winter arrived, more anglers were turning up, some very dedicated ones and with these setting up close by, our results were always going to reflect this, as we were all actually targeting the same fish.

Although I always keep accurate records of each session, I have never been one to keep statistical records, one that logs every 2lb rudd, or any other species for that matter, but an incredible amount of specimen rudd were taken that winter, although, none surpassed the 3lb mark.

During the summer of 2010, my efforts for rudd after dark were somewhat disappointing, yet looking back at previous records, the amount of big rudd taken in the summer months is far fewer than those of the winter ones, and I started to realise that big rudd are actually easier to catch in the winter. The morning tench sessions were incredible, though, with upward of 20 being taken in just a few hours. The standard pattern arose when as summer progressed, results dwindled and I left it until November before a return was made.

A few other specialist anglers had already fished the venue in October and their catch reports in the angling weeklies had drawn far more attention than I had hoped, yet who am I to complain, as I am probably my own worst enemy when it comes to drawing attention to the winter rudd fishing on Frensham.

The weed was also bad and after a plumb around, I found where the weed ended and started to bait up, popping down every other evening after dark, armed with a spod rod plus a kilo of hemp and half a pint of maggots. After around six visits, I returned and straight away started to catch, but it was noticeable how few tench showed compared to previous years. I can only imagine that they were tucked away in the weed keeping warm somewhere, whereas in the past with no weed around they had to eat to keep warm.

Part of the catch that started it all.

At midnight the action slows. Time for a warm bed.

Here are the actual words taken from my diary of one of the sessions:

Frensham Great Pond, Monday 22nd November 2010.

Conditions: Overcast with a slight n/w wind, A/P at 1012mb and temperature ranging between 6 degrees and 2 overnight.
Duration of session: Overnight.

Tactics: Heli-rigs for rudd.
Result: Fifteen rudd to 2lb 12oz, five tench and a 3lb 5oz perch.

Unfortunately, my time in this swim, in fact this area, was short-lived as one evening I noticed an elderly angler fishing further down the bank. Turning down my alarms I proceeded to have an eventful night, yet later that evening I noticed someone behind me and turned to see him walking past. He had obviously clocked my position after hearing a couple of tench splash about. That was it, if I wanted this swim again then I would have to arrive well early in future, yet knowing that the rudd didn't turn on until after dark, I couldn't afford to do this, so I started to bait a few swims further down, which wasn't a problem, apart from the fact that more anglers were arriving.

I can't complain really because a few magazines had requested features on how I was catching winter rudd and as I looked to my left every angler was sending out a small pocket rocket, probably filled with hemp and red maggots before casting out, yep, a helicopter rig. Trying to limit the damage that had by now been done, and trying to keep one step ahead by baiting much further out, I continued to work around these as best I could, but let's face it, anglers are entitled to fish where they like at Frensham.

The nail in the coffin came toward the end of the season when during half term a very mild spell of weather crossed the country. Arriving an hour before dusk, I struggled to park and as I walked up the bank found every swim taken, so I headed for Frensham

Small Pond where all I caught were small roach. I decided there and then to forget Frensham, not just for the remainder of the season but for the whole of the next winter.

The following summer, the weed and blue-green algae was everywhere, yet a plumb around found just four swims toward the main car park to be fishable. The first swim I ever fished at Frensham, and one of my favourites, called the Corridor was fortunately one of these. It required a long walk through a narrow channel between the reeds, it had been kind to me in the past

and didn't let me down this summer. The fishing was incredible with loads of tench being caught on the waggler during the morning and on two occasions the rudd went ballistic with 25 twos falling to waggler tactics in just two short afternoon sessions.

As always, the fishing toughened up as the summer progressed, and with these swims becoming popular due to them being the only ones that were weed-free, I decided to try something different and when Donut suggested mullet, Frensham was forgotten.

The strangest-coloured perch I have ever seen.

Zander

Old Bury Hill

In October 2009, I decided it was time to try to catch a personal best zander and although the River Thames appealed to me, I knew that before embarking on such a difficult campaign I needed to familiarise myself with the species.

My biggest zander, 12lb 13oz, one of 40 that fell over two evenings!

Old Bury Hill in Dorking was the obvious answer, and having already approached its owner David DeVere, back in the summer while filming a video for Korum, I knew that there wouldn't be a problem. Until now, the only zander that I had caught were either small ones while targeting perch at Teddington Weir, along with one of 5lb 4oz that I landed many years prior while fishing a predator match at Old Bury Hill.

The journey to that match seemed to take forever, along the winding A25, passing through the villages of

Gomshall, Abinger Hammer, and Westcott. I wasn't really looking forward to the drive, yet on arrival, was surprised to see that it was no further and took no longer than a trip to the river Loddon.

My timing couldn't have come at a better time as David had been thinking of bringing in a single hook rule, yet needed some statistics and asked if I was interested in helping out. I didn't have to think for long to agree, as in return for forwarding my results and pictures, I could stay late and fish into darkness.

That evening, I headed for what's known as the Grassy Bank, and although it was a fairly slow to start with, the zander seemed to switch on as the light faded, and after fishing a couple of hours into darkness I found myself leaving with six zander to 7lb 7oz, plus a bream. I used small sections of sardine or sprat tails hair-rigged next to a size 8 barbless hook, and just one run was missed.

Another trip was planned for the following week and this time I headed for the shelter of the big oak tree, halfway along the Long Bank, as a storm was brewing. As the session progressed, so did the severity of the storm, and come 10pm, I'd had enough.

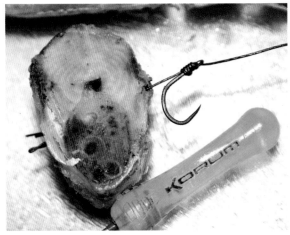

The business end.

Dad's was well happy with his birthday present, a double figured zed.

Overenthusiastic or what!

indicator started to lift and with most fish hooked just within the scissors and having very few hookpulls, it looked as if this was the way forward.

Things got even better as I was allowed to take a paying guest and over the next few months both my dad and Kevin caught zander over 10lb. The statistics spoke for themselves, as probably just one in ten runs was either missed or saw a fish being lost, and with very few being deep hooked, it was inevitable that trebles would be banned come the following season.

Over the next couple of months, I experienced some incredible zander fishing and was extremely fortunate to be allowed to stay into darkness, as it soon became apparent that zander feed hardest just as the light fades, a time when most had to leave. During this period, dozens of zander fell to the single hook and sardine section including one of 10lb 14oz, yet as the winter set in and the frost appeared, sport tailed off considerably and my thoughts once again turned to more obliging species such as perch and chub.

I wasn't able to erect an umbrella, due to the high winds, and with my waterproofs now leaking after being subjected to constant heavy rain, I couldn't continue. Although uncomfortable, the fishing was incredible, the zander must have been turned on by the weather, and I lost count of the zander caught which included a personal best of 10lb 4oz. Once again, almost every run was converted, even after striking as soon as the

The following October I was back, and during the first week fished two evenings taking over 40 zander, including fish of 12lb 12oz and my best, to date, 12lb 13oz. The month of October was incredible, obviously the zander were hungry and were so easy to catch; I even started to fish the waggler and cage feeder for them. It was a fantastic way to fish and anyone who reckons they don't fight wants to hook one on a float or quiver tip rod!

It wasn't just zander that started to feed on the sardine sections. Regular introductions of groundbait laced with cut-up pieces of fish brought the carp and bream into the swim and created a welcome variation. As the water cooled though, so did the sport and come the end of November things became tough again making me turn my attention to other species, yet I had, by now, made a mental note to return in March, as I had a feeling that this might just provide something special, and it did.

The previous summer, I had started to take my first tentative steps into guiding other anglers and it was on such a session that my client, Mark, hooked and landed a massive zander. I remember the night well as it was really cold, so much so that frost covered the unhooking mat. I had two customers that night, Mel and Mark and neither were feeling that confident. They would probably have packed up if it hadn't been for me telling them to have faith and give it until 8pm.

Oh, how I would love a fish like this! Ashley with a Thames monster.

Kevin with a big zander.

A small pike to Mark and a small zander to Mel created some confidence, then at 7pm both anglers found themselves playing fish. Kneeling on the platform, I shone my head torch out into the darkness and watched as Mel's zander surfaced, a fish around 7lb, then I saw Mark's surface, which completely dwarfed Mel's. Quickly apologising to Mel, I slid the net under Mark's, then netted Mel's; however, it wasn't until I tried to lift the bigger of the two that I realised that we had caught something very special. I struggle to estimate zander,

normally my guess is around a pound or more light, and once again this was the case. My estimate of 14 saw the dial racing past this and settling on 16lb 2oz, a new lake record!

Since that day, at least two clients have beaten my personal best zander. Mel, who witnessed the lake record being caught, is one of them and has returned a few times in his quest for a big zander. We have spent numerous hours targeting a variety of specimen fish and although some creditable fish had crossed his net, a really big specimen hadn't, so when he slid the net under another Old Bury Hill monster, justice had been done.

Old Bury Hill is a very special place, without a doubt the best zander day-ticket water in the country, and I have to thank the fishery for letting me become part of this historic venue.

Mark with his lake record of 16lb 2oz, taken on a freezing evening.

The tale of two fifties

CEMEX Angling Species Challenge

In May 2009, CEMEX Angling announced the CEMEX Angling Challenge Cup through the highly informative Carp and Coarse Angler magazine. Competing for the title didn't even cross my mind when it was launched, as it was really aimed at CEMEX Angling Plus members.

At 53lb 4oz she was going to repay me big time.

Sadly, it didn't attract the members as intended, and come September, the competition had only received three catch reports. No entries were shown in the October issue and as my article 'Dairy of a Specimen Angler' was recording what I had been up to in August, no one knew that by this time I had decided to get involved. I had spent the whole of September quietly visiting numerous CEMEX venues targeting different species and submitting them to CEMEX Head Office.

In brief, the competition was a species challenge and required anglers to catch as many of the 17 species listed as they could. These had to be caught from CEMEX venues, witnessed, and then points were awarded on a percentage of the British Record, so if you caught a 2lb 2oz roach you would receive 50 points as the roach record stands at 4lb 4oz.

To be honest, I felt for Mick and Roo who were injecting some well-needed ideas into the establishment, and as their hard work and enthusiasm shone through, it looked like their partnership was going to take the CEMEX empire to a new level and one that would be difficult to match. Unfortunately, it wasn't to be as behind the scenes cuts were being made and something was about to give.

Coming from a match background, I have always been competitive, and although my competitive nature against other anglers had long since left me, I still needed something to thrive on, and this competition fitted my needs perfectly. From September right through to the end of May I set targets to catch as many species as I could, 50 per cent of the record for each was my aim, giving an overall point tally of 850 come the end of the competition. If I could achieve this, I knew that the £3000 payout was fairly secure, yet even though competitors were few, I never once questioned my dedication as this had become a competition against new venues and the fish they held, and while on the journey, I was fortunate to familiarise myself with many of the fantastic CEMEX venues.

In September, I visited venues such as Ellis Pit on the Arlesford Complex, Summer Pit, Papercourt, Frimley, Theale, Yateley Split Lake along with the River Wey and Trent and come the end of the month, I had submitted eight species on the score sheet, totalling 301 points. My diary piece and these captures were published in the November issue, a time when the few other competitors realised that they had a competition on their hands. They also realised that for them, the chance of catching a crucian carp or rudd was gone and that they would have to allocate some of their time by the end of May if they had any hope of catching me up.

It was a game plan that had worked perfectly and a competition that suited my style of angling and I was thoroughly enjoying myself. Come the end of the year, I had increased my point tally to 416, the highlight being an unexpected 4lb 8oz eel that had picked up my maggot hookbait offered on a helicopter rig at Kingsmead, that was intended for roach.

The chilly months of January, February and March saw pike, perch, dace and tench added to the score sheet and by now it seemed that anyone else was fishing for second place, yet with a score of over 550 I was still a long way from my final target, so I headed to CEMEX Split Lake with catfish on my mind.

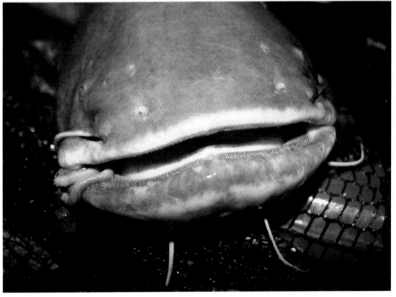

They may be ugly but you have to admire the fight.

The Split Lake bream are also worthy targets.

The following words are taken from my Carp and Coarse diary.

CEMEX Split Lake, Monday 29th March.

Conditions: Wet with a south-westerly but mild at 12 degrees and falling to around six overnight. Water temperature at 12.5 degrees and atmospherics falling from 996mb.

Duration of session: Overnight.

Tactics: Three different set-ups in the hope of a catfish.

Result: Two 8lb bream and a 16lb 8oz common to the boilie and PVA bags of pellet, one aborted run on a sardine section, and three runs on the worms which produced one fish, a 53lb 4oz cat!

The capture of this catfish was unbelievable as it was only my second night on the venue, very early in the year, and on a method that was to reward me again within a few days. The fight was simply awesome. I was using 28lb braid, fishing from the Double Dairy, and struggled to stop the fish from finding the sanctuary of the islands.

Its capture also allowed me some respite, a time when I was able to target species that had already been caught, with the view of increasing their weight, and of course my point tally as well, and Frimley Pit Two didn't disappoint.

The Split Lake catfish fell to a bunch of lobworms popped just six inches off the bottom on a running set-up and its effectiveness needed to be tried out elsewhere. Kevin and his son, Max, were fishing Badshot Lea Big Pond for the evening, so I headed out for a social and just into darkness hooked a fish, once again on braid, that was to beat me up for a good 15 minutes.

I remember the three of us kneeling in the swim, watching what looked like a giant tadpole come swimming past. At the time, the venue was recovering from an unfortunate outbreak of KHV, so we had to land the fish in a landing net that was supplied. How my brother got the catfish in the net I will never know, but somehow he did. On the scales, the needle settled exactly on 57lb, another personal best and was one of three cats that I

landed that night, with a further three lost. Never underestimate what a bunch of lobworm will catch!

The last two months of the competition, April and May, saw a strange twist of fate, one that saw me throwing an expensive syndicate ticket into the bin without even visiting the venue. It was a blessing in disguise, as it pointed me toward Westhampnett in search of bream, and later that month I was lifting a truly magnificent specimen of 15lb 4oz for the camera. The venue also increased my king carp weight to 28lb 14oz and these fish increased my total to 671, less than my target, and one I have to say I was disappointed with, yet it was more than enough to win the Challenge Cup.

Max was speechless when this 57lb catfish was netted.

CHAPTER TWENTY-FOUR

Chub: Saviours of the winter

For some reason, chub have never been a species that I have felt the need to go and target, probably because to me they are the saviours of each winter, ever-willing to feed, even in the harshest of conditions, and for this reason I know that each winter I will be forced to fish for them.

It's never too cold for chub.

I suppose I treat them similar to carp when I'm bream fishing, and just know that a few will be caught while targeting other species, such as barbel. Don't get me wrong, I love chub fishing and find it addictive. I know that if I work a number of swims using breadflake or cheese paste, even on the coldest day, then a bite is almost guaranteed, yet they aren't the hardest of fighters and are fairly predictable. Given that, I have probably caught more specimen chub than any other species, a statistic that proves the point that a sustained campaign isn't required.

When I say 'predictable', I mean that on the rivers I fish, the Loddon and Kennet, after maybe six roving sessions, their haunts can be found and once the river has been learned, I can return knowing which swims I will be visiting. Usually, each swim will provide a bite; however, a bite doesn't always mean a capture, as they can be extremely crafty, especially when spooked.

It's this crafty nature that I love, because if a bite is missed I just know that the next won't be as positive. They will let you know they are around, as they seem to be unable to resist testing the bait and the small pulls and plucks can play mind games and it takes every bit of my angling skill to extract one. Once one has been caught it's time to move on; it fits in with my roving approach perfectly, and has the added bonus of allowing me to learn a river quickly, as well as keeping me warm.

There are swims, especially on the Kennet, that I know can be exploited using large quantities of maggots, yet unlike sitting and working a stillwater swim, this approach has never interested me. The few times I have set out to achieve a result using such a tactic, I find myself becoming bored and not enjoying it; maybe I'm just not patient enough.

The one winter that I did decide to try to catch a seven, was in 2009. I bought a Ringwood and District AA ticket and headed to Throop. That winter was harsh and I found myself travelling down, well before dawn, on roads that were icy and dangerous, and it was this that finally made me think twice. Plenty of chub were caught, yet I was rapidly becoming known as 'the pest controller' and after numerous visits I failed to break the 5lb barrier.

Looking back, I classify the Stour as a man's river, one that you need to dominate, and if you feel intimidated by it, even in the slightest, then it's going to beat you. It's a river I should have given more time to, maybe walking the banks in the summer would have helped, and although the river didn't beat me, travelling down on tenterhooks did.

Even though I arrived early on Throop, only a couple of swims could be fished without distraction, and that was another confidence-drainer. Regular anglers seemed to be masters of frequenting many swims very quickly and knowing that if you're the second angler in a swim it will be ten times harder, finding breadcrumbs in most didn't help. I'm not sure if anglers sprinkled breadcrumbs in the swims to deter others, but finding it did knock my confidence, yet it was a trick I learned the hard way and

now repeat the process on stretches of the Loddon, only this time it works in my favour!

My biggest chub of 7lb 1oz was taken from the Standford End Stretch on the Loddon, and although this may seem massive to many, to a specimen angler it isn't anything exceptional. If I were to dedicate more time to the species and fish the right stretches of river then it wouldn't take long to increase this. Just like bream, a few years ago my best stood at just 10lb 2oz, then the urge came to increase this and the following spring, after fishing a water that held big bream, I increased it to a creditable 15lb 4oz.

How many sixes does it take to catch a seven? A lot!

For now, the roving approach suits me.

Since then, I've taken dozens of bream bigger than 10lb 2oz. In fact, fish of this size are returned without being photographed and it just goes to prove that if you want an 8lb chub, then you have to fish a stretch of river that contains an 8lb chub. If I continue to fish the stretches I do at the moment, which are great for getting the rod bending in the winter, then I will probably never better my existing best.

Here are the words taken from my diary of the day I caught my personal best:

River Loddon, Wednesday 1st December 2010.

Conditions: Absolutely freezing and a brisk north wind creating a wind chill of around minus 4 degrees. A/P at 1006, with slight snow showers.

Duration of session; 11am to 2pm.

Tactics: Breadflake for chub.

Result: Six chub including fish of 5lb 4oz, 5lb 9oz, 5lb 14oz and 7lb 1oz.

One day the urge will come and I will find myself heading, probably to the River Lea, maybe even back to the Stour, but I have many years of angling ahead of me and feel that an 8lb chub is something that I will achieve one day in the future. When that happens, I want it to be caught while dedicating the time to them, and if I had a choice of venue to catch such a fish, then it would have to be the Thames, a river I intend to spend more time on over the next few years.

After-dark barbel sessions on the Kennet are often interrupted by big chub.

The fish I wish I'd never caught, twice!

Frensham Great Pond

It surprises people when they ask me, 'what's the best fish you have ever caught?' and I reply, 'The 31lb 10oz pike taken from Thorpe Park in 2002,' especially when they know I caught the biggest stillwater roach to be taken in the country for many years, not once, but twice.

Explosive tench action at Frensham

Weighing 3lb 15oz 8drams, it was first landed back in February 2010. It came on a wet and windy night when I was targeting specimen rudd using the fantastic helicopter rig baited with two red maggots along with a small piece of foam to pop these off the bottom. It was the only fish of the evening; probably because once I had landed it, I couldn't carry on as I was a nervous wreck. My only witness that evening was my girlfriend, who instantly knew the importance of this fish from my reactions. Although I took close-up photographs of it, I wish now that I had called someone to come down and witness the fish, as I wasn't expecting my honesty and experience to be questioned after the event.

The pictures were sent to the weekly magazines as well as to my good friend Simon Scott at Sparsholt College, whose judgement I trust impeccably. I was convinced of the fish's authenticity but also knew that it would come under some scrutiny, down to its sheer size. The amount of interest that this fish created was beyond anything that I was expecting.

Simon was on the case straight away and after looking at the close-up images, said that he saw no reason to question the roach as anything but a roach - good enough for him is good enough for me! Unbeknown to me, the images of the fish, not the close-ups, were passed on by the weeklies to a number of specialists for their comments, and the feedback was so contrasting it puzzled me. While the Angler's Mail accepted it as a roach based on their expert's diagnosis, and mine, The Angling Times questioned it.

For months, it seemed that this fish was making headlines; some were good, others bad, yet if there was one thing positive that came about from the capture of this fish, it was the proof that you cannot make judgement of a fish simply from a photograph, and that the need for DNA testing is paramount in the future of identifying potential British record fish that have the tendency to hybridise, or so I thought!

I must admit that I was aware of DNA testing prior to catching this roach, but was under the impression that not only was a scale needed but a fin cutting as well. Knowing that these would be detrimental to the fish's welfare, and let's face it, the fish wasn't a British record, I refrained from doing so, especially in an age when we go to extraordinary lengths to protect the fish we catch.

Finally, everything settled down, and the following winter, once again, I found myself enjoying the rudd fishing on Frensham. Almost to the day, a year later, on a wet and windy evening, I was to reacquaint myself with the same fish.

Having spodded a kilo of hemp and dead maggots into position, I cast out and dropped my standard helicopter rigs on to the baited area. An hour passed, and soon after a recast the indicator danced in true rudd fashion. Straight away, I knew that I had hooked a good fish, but the lack of head shaking, characteristic of rudd, and the lack of power normally experienced from tench, had me somewhat perplexed. Finally, a flash of silver hit the surface and amazingly, the same roach dropped into the waiting net.

I have to admit to having mixed emotions at the time, and almost slid her back without weighing or photographing her, but something told me to gather my thoughts and take my time. Once she was safely secured in the net, I sat back, poured a coffee and decided whether or not it was worth going through the same fiasco as before, but it needed to be done, even if I was to prove myself wrong. She looked in a bad way, as if she was coming to the end of her days, with a big fresh sore on one side and unsurprisingly, down in

weight at 3lb 11oz. Removing a scale, I quickly did a self-take before slipping her back and settling down to a fishless further few hours.

The scale was sent to Simon Scott at Sparsholt who agreed to get the necessary people involved, yet after a communication breakdown regarding whether or not DNA could be taken from a scale alone, things went on hold. Simon asked if I wanted the scale returned but I saw little point so he said that he would store it

Happy, but not for long.

away within his box of 'fishy bits'. Luckily, he did this, as while perch fishing a couple of months later, I received a call from Nigel Hewlett of the Environmental Agency enquiring into whether or not I still had the scale. I explained that Simon may still have this and with my permission, Nigel contacted Simon and was sent a rather smelly scale, by all accounts, and he forwarded this to laboratory in the West Country to be DNA checked.

Months passed, then out of the blue, the news came through that the results proved that the fish I caught was 100% roach. Did I get the Champagne out? No, as by then the confusion that this fish had left me in, and the angling world, had overrun any emotions within me.

This was the fish I wish I'd never caught, and it was the fish that saw my outlook on angling take a different direction. Angling is to be enjoyed, that is the most important factor, and although I will continue to look at catching big fish as this is what drives me on, there seems little point in publishing every fish I catch.
This roach should be far beyond any fish I have ever caught, yet to think about it or talk about it brings me no joy whatsoever and should have deserved a chapter far longer within my book, but ends up with just a few paragraphs. Says it all, really.

It's amazing how one fish brought so much happiness and turned me into a specimen angler, but a decade or so later, an even bigger one created the opposite feeling.

Catching fish is to be enjoyed. Never forget this!

Two fourteens!

Burghfield

I was first introduced to this stretch of the river on March 13th 2003 by Blobby, and that day I was fortunate to catch a personal best chub weighing 5lb 8oz, which fell to a lobworm in a swim that I later found out to be the best chub swim on the stretch. Later that year, I returned, this time in search of another species that this stretch has become famous for, barbel.

I remember the day well. It was early afternoon and Neil Wayte was guiding me by mobile phone to the banker swim, at that time. Gary Newman had briefed me on tactics which were to bait-drop eight loads of maggot and hemp to the far bank reeds, leave for 15 minutes, and then cast a maggot feeder across, baited with a single hair-rigged rubber caster which had two real ones superglued either side. If nothing happened then I needed to repeat the process over the course of the afternoon, which I did.

Back then, there was no night fishing on the stretch and members had to be off the water at dusk, dependant on time of year, and today it was at 7.30pm. Nothing happened all afternoon and I remember looking at the watch when it was 7.29pm. As I turned round, the tip tapped, pulled over and after a less-than-spectacular fight, a personal best barbel weighing 10lb 15oz sat in the net.

Two trips, two personal bests, you would have thought that this was the catalyst to a long-lasting relationship with the river, yet it wasn't to be, and I stuck with my local River Loddon, a river that I had grown up on.

I have always thought the fish in Burghfield to be 'food fish', mainly due to the stretch being extremely pressured and plenty of bait being deposited within it. In the past, anglers could fish the stretch on a relatively cheap CEMEX Angling ticket and with no night fishing allowed, these big fish could go on a feeding spree after dark then sit up during the daylight hours, making them very difficult to catch.

Over the last few seasons, CEMEX Angling have, much to the disappointment of many, syndicated the stretch and allowed night fishing, so these huge barbel and chub now have no escape and can be targeted 24/7, and being accustomed to anglers' bait need to feed, yet with far fewer anglers on the stretch, it means the chance of bumping into one of these monsters has been greatly increased.

Since syndication, I have dabbled with the stretch, taking barbel to just over 12lb and chub to over six, yet even now, with the banks relatively quiet and the stretch still containing a good head of very big fish, it's a place I have never really warmed to or felt the desire to concentrate on full time.

Why this is, I don't know, maybe it's that I just don't know the stretch as well as I do certain parts of the Loddon and always felt that my style of angling, which, in brief, is short bursts in favourable conditions, never fitted in here, but this is all changing and the call of the Kennet is now beginning to encourage me back, more and more.

When the phone rang and it was Mick at Sky Sports asking if I was up for a Tight Lines feature, I agreed, as always, yet when he said they were looking at catching a specimen autumnal barbel, I sat back and questioned what I had done.

The easy option would have been to head to the Loddon, but I felt that viewers would only ask questions about my versatility and I thought it would be good for my profile to head somewhere new.

Burghfield has always been kind to me, especially considering the hours I've put in so this seemed the obvious answer and always willing to promote CEMEX Angling, I made arrangements to meet the film crew in The Cunning Man car park at dawn. The conditions were far from favourable. After a chilly start, the mist cleared leaving a brilliant blue sky, warm sunshine and little in the way of breeze. My confidence wasn't sky high as I walked along the Kennet and Avon canal, but I knew that if I could keep on the move and search the stretch then maybe the fishing gods would smile and bless me. I had also looked at the barometer as I left home and it signalled a brief wet spell moving in during the afternoon but would it arrive in time?

The Snag swim was my first choice as it provided cover from the sunshine but after an hour and a half the tip remained motionless, time to move. The next three hours or so was spent dropping in different swims, spending 40 minutes in each, before settling back in the Snags. Andy Ford was the producer on the day and as we spoke something happened, but it was so fast we both questioned what.

Caught for the cameras, at 14lb 2oz.

I can see them, but can I catch them?

All we saw was the tip of the rod fly backwards, it was that quick, but it was the signal I needed and as I looked skyward, the blue was beginning to be replaced with heavy grey clouds.

Although I felt the need to move again, I had a feeling that this swim would produce, so in order to save the swim for a final cast before darkness, I left Andy to guard it but not before priming it with a few small balls of scalded pellet.

The reliable chub swim upstream failed to produce and back in the snags, one more cast was made. Looking at the sky it really was a question whether we would get a bite before the heavens opened, but with the light levels dropping by the second, my confidence rose. What was noticed first was just the odd ring around the line that entered the water; fish were in the swim. However, when the tip pulled round, my strike met thin air and I kicked myself at being so eager, as it had to be a liner.

Worried that I had blown my chance, I made another cast and watched for what seemed an eternity before the next liner came. Relaxing, I held the rod, knowing that the damage caused from striking earlier hadn't been fatal and that the inevitable was going to happen. The size of the liners grew, some moving the tip a good foot, then the next thing I knew, I was hanging on for dear life. This was one hell of a brute as it fought hard downstream before swimming past, ripping line of a tight clutch as it headed upstream, but my tackle slowly sapped its energy and after a defiant slap of its tail, it drifted slowly over the drawstring.

Words are not enough to explain the wonderful feeling that was flowing through my veins at that moment but I was one very happy and relieved angler. Andy mentioned that after watching the bite, he fully expected to hear a splash and see the soles of my shoes disappearing underwater.

Weighing 14lb 2oz, it was my biggest barbel from the Kennet and as I slipped her back, I knew that this fish rated right up there with any I'd ever caught, it meant that much.

The following week, I returned, and below are the words taken from my diary:
River Kennet, Monday 14th Novemebr 2011.

I have a feeling the big barbel are shoaled up in the snags as the liners I received last week before catching for Sky couldn't have been from just one fish, they were far too frequent.

My sixth sense once again told me to grab the barbel tackle and, ignoring everything else, I headed back to Burghfield in the hope that the same swim was free. The weather felt really good, with cloud cover, a slight S/W wind and A/P reading a favourable 998mb.

The Snags swim was free so I decided to sit it out for three hours, and to cast the method-lead in for the first hour, then if nothing happened, to introduce some free offerings and sit for the next hour with a big walnut-sized piece of paste, repeating this for the final hour. If I got liners toward the end of the three hours, then I would stay a while longer, but if nothing happened I'd call it a day.

The first hour passed without incident, so I made another cast. I checked my watch, it was approaching 5pm and darkness was falling. After 20 minutes, I felt myself dropping-off so I reduced the drag on the reel; that should wake me up if I received a take. Sure enough, a click of the clutch had me looking and in true barbel fashion, the tip pulled round.

At first, I thought that I'd hooked a big chub because it held its ground without the expected barbel surge downstream, and I was able to start pumping the fish

upstream. As the weight on the other end increased I assumed that it would be a modest barbel but when the fish passed me and headed upstream, I realised that I was attached to something special.

In the net, it was a far longer fish than that of the previous week and I noticed the wart on the tail root, indicating that it was one of the big girls. It weighed 14lb 11oz, and I was absolutely blown away. In less than a week, a method that some said would never work on the Kennet had taken two big fish.

My biggest barbel from the Kennet, weighing 14lb 11oz.

It wasn't to end there. Just days later I was back, this time testing a rod out for an Angler's Mail feature and within minutes of casting out, the tip flew round and another big Burghfield barbel graced my net, this time weighing 12lb 1oz.

The method-lead is a tactic in which I have complete faith; faith creates confidence and along with these two, there is just one other factor, time.

The method-lead - deadly.

A needle in a haystack

Gold Valley

After the stressful series of events following the capture and diagnosis of my massive roach, the last thing I really wanted to get involved with was another 'is it, or isn't it?' situation, yet after setting a precedent, that's exactly what I found myself doing.

I had noticed a picture published in Angler's Mail of a very big crucian that had been caught during a match on the Middle Lake at Gold Valley. This complex of lakes is almost on my doorstep, and my first impressions, from the relatively poor picture, was that the fish looked very much like the real deal.

I have always had a passion for one of our country's most frustrating of species, from my early days catching them as a child at Hartley Mauditt Pond, to more recently, targeting a potential British Record, at CEMEX Angling's Little Moulsham. I have to admit it, my eyebrows were raised when I saw the picture, but I resisted the temptation to target this fish, as the title 'specimen hunter' has never sat comfortably with what I classify myself as, an all-rounder specialist angler, and if I were to try to catch this fish, then that's exactly what I would become.

A couple of months passed before this fish cropped up in a conversation. I was the guest appearing with Keith Arthur on Tight Lines and it was just before broadcasting that Keith asked if I had seen this fish and what my thoughts were on it. We agreed that it looked like a real crucian, and Keith gave me a challenge to catch and identify the fish, and anyone who knows me, will agree that I like a challenge.

When I arrived at Gold Valley a few days later, I think John Raison was already expecting my visit and granted permission for me to fish the middle lake whenever I wished. It was just three minutes drive from my home and seemed perfect for a few short sessions when the time presented itself. It was also a great venue for my father and girlfriend's dad to join me, as a good chat along with a few fish, would make their day.

Both Keith and John had mentioned that whenever the crucian had been caught, it had come from the area between the two life buoys on the right-hand bank, so why try anywhere else? I already knew the tactic I would use prior to my first visit in early August, which was the method-lead, a tactic that had worked wherever I had taken it, and I knew that if this fish picked up my bait, then it would almost certainly find the bottom of my landing net. Crucians love the margins, so there was no need to fish any further than a rod length out, and in doing so I hoped that this would keep the bream and carp at bay.

Before I continue, let me explain the method-lead as most have associated this as an over-gunned bolt-rig. In simple terms, the rig consists of a one-ounce inline lead that runs freely on a 6lb main line. This lead is buffeted by a Quick-change bead onto which a three-inch hooklink is attached, made from 4lb fluorocarbon. On the end of this is a size 16 hook, tied knotless knot-style to leave a short hair. Corn or pellet is usually the bait and around the lead a good helping of Sonubaits Super Crush Green is pressed.

No freebies are added to the well-sieved groundbait and after swinging into position the groundbait forms a carpet on the lake bed with your hookbait sitting bang in the middle, looking similar to the cherry on the cake. It's a method that is maybe frowned on, but that's because it has been misunderstood, and looking at the biggest crucians that appear on the British Record list, most have been caught using similar tactics, although most anglers aren't aware of this.

The first session was a real eye-opener and one that made me realise just what I had let myself in for, as after catching almost every species in the lake, and dozens of them, I knew this was to be the ultimate, needle in a haystack.

I think it was during my third session that I finally hooked and landed my first crucian, one of around 2lb and looking at this fish in the flesh, I had absolutely no reason to doubt its authenticity. Old-looking with tatty fins, no barbules and buttery-coloured in appearance, everything fell in with what I was looking for.

Over the next couple of months, I tried to fish the lake at least once a week, sometimes twice, and come early October my tally of fish exceeded 700. Out of this I managed nine crucians, and every one was of a similar size to the first. I even decided to fish a night, but come 1am, and after taking dozens of hard-fighting carp, decided enough was enough and wound in to get some sleep.

Gold does have crucians in it.

To be honest, by October, thoughts of actually catching this fish were beginning to slip away, and I had almost resigned myself to an early spring campaign the following year, yet on October the 9th, while fishing with my dad, things changed.

Setting up in our normal position, with a ripple pushing from left to right, I found myself struggling for bites, even though I was using two rods. Dad was to my right and was giving me a real beating up using just one rod, so I wound in, walked over, poured a cup of tea and watched as he slaughtered the swim. I remember tying up a new hooklink for him, as the one he was using was kinked from catching so many fish.

He was also using punched luncheon meat as opposed to the usual sweetcorn, something he had failed to tell me earlier in the day.

The next bite almost pulled the rod in, and as Dad bent into what was thought to be another carp, you could see that he was taking no prisoners. Then the fish surfaced and he went from giving it some serious stick to playing it with kid gloves, as what surfaced was the fish we had been targeting. Squeaky bum, jelly legs, you name it, we were both feeling it, but after what seemed ages I stretched out and engulfed the fish within the mesh. Looking in the net, this fish looked huge and high fives, handshakes; even a cuddle followed the capture.

Go on, give it some stick, Mick!

The needle in the haystack.

The only way to find out.

waiting, I spent some time looking at the fish's credentials; fin ray count, lateral line scale count, you name it, and every detail fitted into place, so there was no reason to doubt its authenticity, apart from my own gut feelings. I requested permission to remove a scale so that it could be DNA tested for a positive identification, and this was agreed.

That day, the scale was on its way to Nigel Hewlett at the Environmental Agency who had kindly agreed to finance the DNA testing. Almost five months passed before the email arrived detailing the DNA test findings, and although I was hopeful of it being 100% crucian, I wasn't confident, and if I were a betting man, then I would have been right, as the diagnostic didn't go in our favour.

These are the actual words received back on the results:
'The sample has been run through two independent processes which confirm that the scale you sent has the genetic fingerprint of a F1 hybrid. For each of the six markers it shows diagnostic alleles for both crucian carp and goldfish.'

Although Dad didn't show it, I'm sure he was disappointed, as were John and Keith. However,

Although Dad had no reason to doubt its pedigree, I soon had misgivings, mainly due to its colour, as this fish was far darker than the smaller crucians that I'd caught in previous sessions, but not wanting to spoil the moment, I kept my feelings to myself. I called my brother, who is also passionate about crucians, and his feelings, when seeing the fish were the same as mine, yet everyone else around seemed adamant that what they were looking at was a new British record crucian. Carefully zeroing the scales, we lifted her skywards and watched as the needle swung past the 5lb, finally settling between the four and five-ounce mark!

It was now time to get it witnessed and as this could be a history-making fish, I thought it only fair that the Tight Lines film crew be called to record its capture. While considering the amount of fish in the lake, for my father to actually go in search of this fish and to catch it has to be applauded, as it was a magnificent achievement and one for which I'm very proud of him.

It also goes to show that a fish should never be judged on photographic evidence alone, especially a species with tendencies to hybridise, something I have mentioned before. If it's a fish of significant value to the history of angling in this country, or one that could potentially become a British Record, then the only way to get a positive identification is to get it DNA tested. Anyone who accepts, or identifies a fish, on photographic evidence alone, is either very brave or taking a big risk!

Tarn; another crucian venue dismissed.

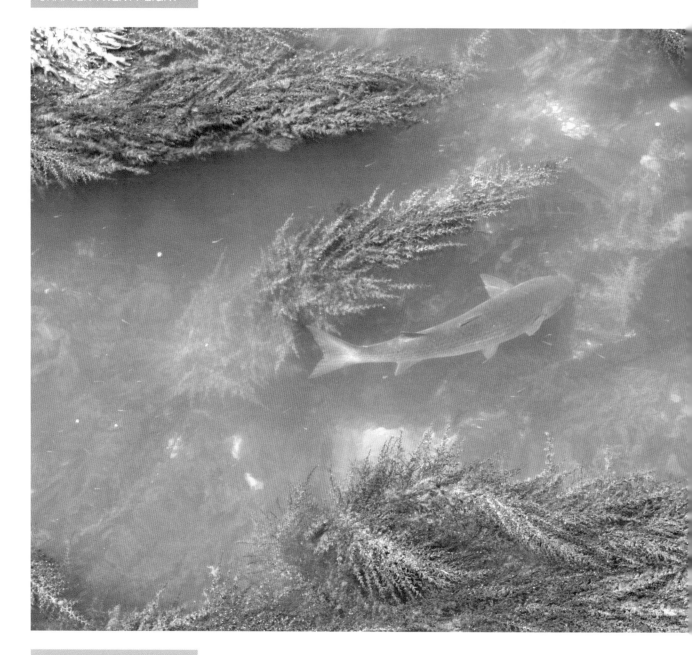

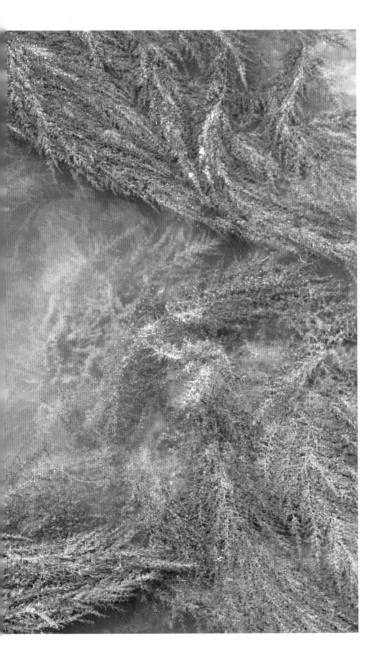

Mullet madness

Every now and again I need to remove myself from the specimen world, as it's all too easy to get obsessed with a target, and I've learned over the years that if it's not happening, then sometimes a complete change is needed. I could easily have returned to the Thames in search of carp, but with the guiding business taking off in a big way, I rarely found two consecutive days to fish, something you need to have if you are to get the best from such a big river.

Donut had started to get back into fly fishing and had tried to tempt me out on numerous occasions but I knew that the constant casting would only aggravate an old shoulder injury. However, when he emailed a picture of a 3lb 13oz thick-lipped mullet, it grabbed my attention and before long we were making our way south to the River Arun in search of this frustrating species.

It was like a breath of fresh air, a new adventure, and as we made our way through the picturesque countryside of Hampshire and West Sussex, and over the mist-shrouded South Downs, our excitement heightened. Donut relived his capture from the previous week and built a picture in my head of massive mullet slurping down pieces of bread that were thrown in off the harbour wall for the swans. It was a scene that I wanted to witness for myself, yet for me, today wasn't about catching, and I had already decided that I wouldn't cast a line until Donut had caught.

It was still dark when we arrived in Littlehampton and as we made our way to the harbour entrance, Donut's pace increased. Looking over the edge, we could see that our arrival was perfect, the tide was still heading seawards and come first light would have slowed enough to make fishing possible. Our arrival wasn't missed by the swans, which were now heading in their hundreds towards us from every direction in the hope of an early meal, and I asked Donut how he ever managed to catch with them around. It was then that I realised that it takes two to catch a mullet from this position; one to feed the swans, keeping them interested upstream, while the other would try to spot a mullet and cast to it in the hope that it would take, before one of its feathery friends barged in.

As the light grew, we peered into the clearing water, which was some 15 feet down. At first, no mullet were spotted, then as I looked downstream a dorsal fin hit the surface, followed by another and as we hurried down we could make out three thick-lipped mullet, the best probably approaching 6lb. I knew what to do and moved upstream with a couple of slices of bread to feed the swans, hoping to create a brief window of opportunity for Donut to make a cast. I watched as he flicked his free-lined breadflake out and teased it in so it slowly fell in front of the mullet, then the next thing I remember was watching his carp rod arch over and hearing the clutch scream as an angry mullet headed out into the flow.

I watched as the fish headed out into the centre of the river with Donut struggling to stay in contact, but then his line fell slack as the hook pulled. Donut knew he had just lost a specimen mullet and although I could see his disappointment, I reassured him that he would get another chance.

My initial feeling was that this was going to be easy, yet an hour later we were still trying to locate another fish that looked interested. The odd fish was spotted but all were further out, only showing themselves briefly before drifting into deeper water. A passer-by had mentioned that there was a group of mullet further down, almost at the end of the harbour wall, so we made our way down and found them, once again by them showing their dorsal fins, yet as soon as any bread drifted across their heads they were gone.

Donut, with a 4lb 12oz mullet hooked from a bridge, 20 or more feet above the water.

Donut, with a mullet taken from the harbour wall.

that I saw Donut press a small piece of bread onto his hook and remember saying, "Hang on, how you going to land it if you hook one?" His reply was, "That's your problem, mate!"

The mullet below weren't as big as those in the harbour, probably the best around 3lb 8oz and with them taking every piece of bread without fear, we knew that we were about to have a problem and sure enough, first cast saw Donut bent into a fish. I looked at Donut shaking my head, not for the first time I might say, yet he kicked the landing net towards me and pointed to the shore.

"You're joking!"

"No." So I set off, not relishing what was to follow.

Jumping the fence that had a 'do not enter' sign on it, I initially slipped towards the shore, then slowly started to sink before I found myself ankle deep, not happy, but with a mullet in the net, that by now had grown somewhat. I remember looking up and seeing Donut bent over the bridge, punching the air and giggling. Finally being able to control himself he asked, "How big is it?"

"If you want to know, then you'd better come down here and bring the camera with you."

We headed back to our original position but it was obvious that we were wasting our time, so decided to take a walk upstream to try to locate some fish which we finally did below the footbridge. These fish, just like the first, were well active and seemed interested, yet here we were some 20 or more feet up, looking down on a group of fish, easily catchable but with no way of landing them as the rope on the drop net was too short and the shore covered in thick, black mud. It was then

Donut is quite a bit bigger than me, so my amusement started when he struggled to get over the fence, then started sinking in the mud, but when he arrived he was completely surprised, as the mullet on the scales registered a weight of 4lb 12oz. I then reminded him of the one he'd lost earlier and that if we had underestimated this one by such a large margin, then we'd probably underestimated that one as well. I almost felt the lump in Donut's throat at that moment.

The opposite end of the bridge saw more mullet, one that was huge, and we watched with interest as she turned side-on to a moored boat and removed the silkweed from its hull. Others drifted in and out of a concrete structure which was impossible to cast to, and as I looked over the opposite side I spotted a big fish in the edge. Casting well above, I managed to draw my breadflake back so it drifted right past the mullet's nose, yet this was ignored time and time again and after a few minutes we realised that this wasn't a big mullet, but actually a big bass!

Heading upstream, we came across a marina and even from a long way off, could see vortexes on the surface from what could only be mullet, and lots of them, but the signs were there, 'no fishing'. We thought we would go and have a look only to be pounced on by the owner, who said, "Sorry guys. You can't fish in the marina because they are spawning grounds."

Donut mentioned that he thought mullet spawned in Scandinavia and that this was just a reason to stop people fishing, yet as we watched the mullet, they seemed to be chasing each other, similar to other species that are in fact spawning and when one discharged a milky-looking substance from its vent we felt that the owner might have a point.

Harbour action.

Wherever we looked, we saw mullet.

fluorocarbon hooklink, yet I needn't have worried as shortly afterwards, Donut was slipping the net under my first-ever mullet, somewhat smaller than the three that had been circling my bait, but at 2lb 15oz, I wasn't going to complain.

Having covered many miles of river we decided to head slowly back to our original position. By the time we arrived, it was eight o'clock and with the tide now having dropped, Donut soon spotted a few mullet. Once again, the swans were distracted

Moving upstream to the edge of the marina and next to the road bridge, we located a few more and this time I felt far more confident as I was able to trot a float down to the fish; however, after an hour they seem to ignore whatever was presented to them. It was high tide now and the water gin-clear, so I decided to fish over depth and place a lump of flake on the bottom.

Soon after, I had three big mullet circling over the top, obviously interested, and knew that it was just a matter of time before one felt the urge to suck it in. As I watched I noticed a movement to my left and within the blink of an eye another mullet had shot in, picked the flake up and was now heading out into the river.

At first I was somewhat anxious as I was using a Korum 12ft Neoteric float rod and had just tied on a 4.84lb

and a cast was made, and moments later Donut was holding his second mullet, this one weighing 3lb 12oz. After returning the mullet it was noticed how every other fish disappeared, not just from that spot, but throughout the whole of the harbour length, a distance of at least 500 yards. It was as if they had been warned.

We had a couple more trips to Littlehampton that summer but none were as rewarding as the first one, the highlight being me catching a golden grey mullet of 1lb 7oz. The summer was rapidly disappearing and with it so were the mullet, yet during our visits we located some massive mullet plus lots of other spots, not just on the Arun but all along the south coast, in marinas and within estuaries, so come summer next year we will have a great head start, and who knows one of those monsters might just see a landing net.

A personal best golden grey of 1lb 7oz.

Westhampnett revisited

CEMEX Angling Westhampnett

Westhampnett was never forgotten. Those two springs had been etched within my brain and although I longed to return, I had to wait a few years before my next chance came. Ian's departure from RMC, now CEMEX, Angling saw Mick Barnes taking over and meeting Mick while carp fishing a Farnham Angling Society club water many years before had seen a friendship form.

Mick was keen to inject a new direction into the way anglers thought of CEMEX Angling venues, as he knew most felt that they were all-out carp venues, with little else to offer. This was so far from the truth and he asked if I was interested in getting involved to promote this. As you can imagine, I jumped at the opportunity.

The first year, I was only given a coverall permit and this gave me access to numerous venues including the river Kennet at Burghfield, but it was Gold venues such as Little Moulsham and Westhampnett that I was eager to fish. I was promised a Gold Card if I proved my worth and worked relentlessly, completing over 30 articles in the 2007/8 season. It was enough for a Gold Card to be issued and suddenly, I found myself with an endless list of quality venues at my disposal.

Having a portfolio of waters to fish, I needed to prioritise my angling. Although my personal best bream only stood at 10lb 2oz, they weren't that high on my target list at the time, and knowing that Little Moulsham's crucian population were slowly dying out, I knew this was where I needed to concentrate during the summer of 2008. I had also decided to compete for the CEMEX Angling Species Challenge in September 2009, so any sustained campaign targeting a certain species had to be placed on the back burner.

It was while I was in my local tackle shop that I overheard a conversation regarding Westhampnett and that a big hit of large perch had just been caught. Obviously, my ears pricked up and although we were going through a gruelling winter, which saw most venues frozen, I made plans to investigate as soon as

the bad weather eased. I also needed a good perch for the CEMEX Angling Species Challenge that I was competing for. I was somewhat annoyed with myself as I thought that the venue would be frozen, like most others, but I later found out that due to the River Lavant flowing through the venue, it very rarely freezes, so I could have investigated it earlier.

Knowing the venue well, I assumed that the last place the perch would have shoaled up would be the Rutland end, as this was the coldest spot due to the easterly wind blowing into it, so it was the last place I looked. Walking around the pit, I found no clues whatsoever to give me a starting point, that was until I finally unlocked the gate at the Rutland end and found two worn swims.

Looking closer at these, I found the bankstick holes of three separate rods, all pointing in slightly different directions. It was almost certainly the swim that was producing perch, yet what finally confirmed this was a fluorocarbon hooklink left on the ground. No carp angler would dare to use such a frail hooklink and would almost certainly not have his rods on separate sticks. I had located where the perch were coming from by simply looking at the swims, and planned to return a few days later.

The Rutland bank is home to just four swims, numbers 1 to 4, and it was numbers 2 and 3 that were being fished. Respecting the anglers that had found these, and not wanting to tread on their shoes I settled in peg 1. The first two sessions saw three perch caught, the best weighing 2lb 6oz; but, it was during an overnight session when Westhampnett started to reveal its true potential.

The bream fishing begins.

Here are the actual words taken from my diary:
Westhampnett, Monday 25th January 2010.

Conditions: 1038mb, overcast but clearing overnight. Water temperature at 6.8 and the air temperature ranging between four and minus two, however, the north-east wind created a wind chill more like minus five!
Duration of session: Overnight.
Tactics: Maggot feeders with lobworm hookbait.
Result: Three perch, 1lb 13oz, 2lb 15oz and 3lb 9oz, plus a tench of around 4lb!

This should have been the start of a sustained campaign, but I had a couple of other species to catch, so although not forgotten, I moved on with the hope that if my CEMEX Angling ticket was renewed, I could come back the following winter.

A couple of months passed and it was while looking through the weekly angling magazines that I saw a massive bream which had been caught from a lake on the Wasing Estate, in Berkshire. Syndicate places were limited but available and I had to make a decision quickly so I sent a cheque of for £175 to secure my ticket.

It seemed that every other specimen bream angler in the country had the same idea, but this wasn't a problem, in fact a few were very good friends. I was really looking forward to a new challenge, but news came through that the membership included two anglers who had perfected the art of rotating swims between them, and not wanting to be another victim of circumstance, I threw my £175 permit in the bin before even setting eyes on the venue.

More points for the CEMEX Angling Species Challenge.

I'd been getting regular updates on how the lake was fishing from my good friend, Adrian Eves, and in a strange way I was glad to hear that it was extremely tough. Then news came through that it had all gone off during the final week on the venue. It wasn't the bream that had got their heads down, though. The anglers were complaining because, yes, you've guessed it, the way swims were being rotated and stitched up between certain people.

It was at this moment that I knew I had made the right decision, yet I was at a loose end. Then, on reading

an article within the fantastic CEMEX Angling Carp and Coarse Magazine, I noticed that the bream, that had been such rare visitors to the bank at Westhampnett, had started to show. Although the ones being caught weren't anywhere near the size caught from the Wasing Estate, they weren't far off and remembering the shoal I had spotted some years ago, I knew this was where I had to go.

It was May 12th 2010 when I finally returned to Westhampnett. Thoughts now were on bream, and due to throwing my Wasing ticket in the bin, I knew that to compensate for such a drastic measure, I needed to give the campaign everything I had.

The first swim I fished was peg 17, the same swim that I had initially set up in on my first visit with Blobby so many years before, and once again it was a poor swim choice. The reason for choosing it was that I knew it was popular and one that had produced bream prior to my arrival, yet I should have followed my instincts and used the watercraft my father had taught me and followed the wind!

Westhampnett is an 80-acre gravel pit, and although connected, it's divided into two almost identical sections by a pair of splits that extend out into the pit.

Saying that, the distance from one split to the other has to be around 200 yards. Peg 17 looks west, yet take around 20 strides directly behind and you come to peg 15 that looks east, and it was here that, after depositing around 100 balls of groundbait into peg 17, I spotted loads of fish moving, including bream.

Back in my swim, and almost out of bait, I watched the water for hours, only to see one carp crash. I decided to stay put in the hope that any bream in the area would drop down and start feeding, but although I received liners constantly throughout the night, I assumed that these were fish moving on the wind, as come the morning I was totally knackered and fishless.

Dawn in my favourite swim, the Social.

This strange-looking ornamental graces my net every spring.

and set up on the right-hand side as this allowed me to fish the area where I expected the fish to be.

Rules had been changed since my earlier visits, with the rod limit down to three, which I have to admit is enough. I had used fluorocarbon hooklinks on my first visit, so I decided to change one rod over to braid, as although I felt the liners were from moving fish, still felt that I should have got a bite or two. After finding a soft spot directly at the back of a small gravel bar, I set about launching 100 balls of groundbait into position. This spot was at a range of around 100 yards, a distance that I would say is at my limit if I want to fish effectively.

With all the rods clipped up and cast into position, I settled back and awaited a response, which wasn't long in coming from a bream weighing 8lb 1oz. Six more followed during the night, the best going 8lb 12oz, along with a strange ornamental carp and, come morning, I realised that I'd made another mistake, or maybe it was a lesson learned, as all but one fish had fallen to the braided hooklink.

I smiled as I drove home, even though I was disappointed with myself. I had made a foolish mistake but was happy that I had, because I immediately knew that these fish were wind orientated and predictable. They say, 'the best way to learn is from your mistakes', and in angling this rings true.

Two days later I was back, and as soon as I saw that the wind was from the south-west I knew I needed to be fishing in the section situated at the eastern end. There were a few anglers already set up, but with the smaller of the two points free, I made the walk up the road bank

As I packed up and made my way back to the car along the M27 pathway, the angler who had fished the swim where Blobby had pinched the mid-20 carp, stopped me to ask how I had fared. Obviously, he had seen the World War III groundbait bombardment the previous evening and knew I was targeting the bream, so when he congratulated me for catching eight I was somewhat taken back. However when I mentioned the best was just shy of 9lb, he looked at me in amazement, as he had landed two that night while targeting carp, they weighed 13lb and 15lb! He then remarked how he would have happily swapped these for my ornamental carp; likewise! Somewhat gutted at being classified as 'the Westhampnett pest controller', I consoled myself as I drove home. Last night had been a complete success, and although my bream were far smaller than average, I now knew that the size of bream I desired was right there in front of me.

A specimen angler's dream.

It wasn't unusual to catch two doubles at once.

I returned a few days later with the bit between my teeth and set up in another swim, this time in one known as the Social swim. Amazingly, at the time it seemed unpopular with the carp anglers, which suited me as it's situated in the north-east section of the lake, a good hundred yards up the north bank from the corner. Once again, after finding a suitable spot the baiting ritual commenced and I sat back awaiting the response. I knew it would come because the wind was pushing into the corner to my left, and with all rigs baited with critically-balanced corn stacks on braided hooklinks it was just a matter of time. Come the morning, nine bream had graced my net including two doubles. They weighed 10lb 15oz and 13lb 3oz, a new personal best, as well as a couple of upper-double figure carp that I knew had attracted some attention.

Here are the words taken from my diary that had now become a monthly article within Carp and Coarse Monthly:
CEMEX Angling Westhampnett, Tuesday 18th May.

Conditions: A south-west wind with highs reaching 20 degrees and a mild, misty night. High pressure continues at 1032mb. Duration of session: Overnight.

Tactics: Method-lead and corn stacks for bream.
Result: Thirteen bream including six doubles, 10lb 8oz, 11lb 2oz, 11lb 15oz, 12lb 9oz, 13lb 1oz and another PB of 15lb 4oz! Oh, and another carp!

Every session after this followed in a similar fashion with numerous bream to 14lb 4oz and carp to 28lb 14oz landed. Come the start of June, and with the bream beginning to spawn, I decided to move on, yet during this spring not one session saw a blank recorded. I had learned from that initial mistake and taken my father's precious words, 'follow the wind, son!'

It was this season, and this venue, that changed my whole outlook on syndicates, as the group of anglers on this venue were truly amazing. Every time I landed a carp, I could see them watching with their binoculars, probably saying words like, 'That bloody bream angler's just gone and landed another carp!' Little did they know that I had noticed they were watching and had lifted a mid-double out of the water as if it was a 30. I positioned myself for a self-take so they couldn't see the size of the carp, and continued to take a few more before releasing the carp and punching the air, as if in complete jubilation. It wasn't long before the first carp angler entered the swim to enquire what I had caught; the events unfolded, and from that day on I shared a great relationship with the carpers on this water.

Summer, autumn and the first couple of months of winter 2010 passed with my time being spent elsewhere. Perch were on my mind come the winter, and I had already made a long journey to a lake in Kent in the hope of beating my personal best that stood at 4lb 9oz 8drams.

Just how big will this one grow?

Corn stacks fooled this near-30.

One of two 20s caught at the same time.

Unfortunately when I arrived, well before dawn, I found that overnight rain had flooded the venue and after fishing hard until after dark, drove home with just two four-ounce perch to show for my efforts. Thoughts of making these trips on a regular basis wasn't one I looked forward to, and when I weighed up the cost, effort and time involved in breaking my best, I finally decided it wasn't for me. The relatively unknown potential of Westhampnett seemed far more appealing.

It was early February 2011 when I finally got myself sorted and decided to leave the rudd at Frensham alone. Others were following in my footsteps and with the banks becoming busy I needed a new challenge. Dad was to join me and after dropping my van off for an MOT en route, we travelled down together, Dad relaxing in the passenger seat as I drove his Astra.

Dad's car is slightly lower than the standard Astra and the entrance to Westhampnett from the Rutland end was decidedly uneven, to say the least, and as I entered I could hear the underside grating on the kerb. I manoeuvred the car further to the right and the grating ceased, yet stretching to see over the bonnet my foot slipped of the clutch, catapulting the car forward.

Then the problems started, and when I tried to reverse, the wheels span and the car remained in position because a sawn-off tree stump had managed to lodge itself behind the bracket holding the car horn.

Luckily, Matt, the head bailiff, arrived with a bow saw and we soon had the stump removed. However, we had failed to spot the brambles that were trapped in the car's spoiler.

Dawn after a very cold, eel trial session.

The bent spoiler was forgotten for a moment.

On reversing the car, there was a further loud noise, and hanging from the front of the car was Dad's spoiler! Ouch. Amazingly, we decided to fish, albeit a couple of hours later than we would have hoped, and well past the best feeding spell. It was a period which saw little conversation.

No action came to our rods, which was even worse, so I eventually plucked up courage to see if Dad was up for moving to another swim further up the bank. In the new swim, and fishing three rods between us, action wasn't long in coming and amazingly, Dad allowed me to take the first run which resulted in a 3lb perch. The action continued until early afternoon and when we decided to pack away Dad had taken four perch to my three, including a personal best of 3lb 8oz. I questioned how he had caught four to my three and he smiled muttering the words, "Son, you still have a lot to learn."

After so many threes, the four had to come.

That winter a further 12 sessions were crammed in before the perch drifted off to spawn in mid-March. During this time, we managed dozens of perch with a high percentage over 3lb, including one four of 4lb 2oz. The fishing was amazing, and both Dad and Kevin increased their best, with perch well into the 3lb bracket. What made the perch fishing more appealing was that with the water being so clear, every perch was brightly coloured, unlike the washed-out monsters found in murky commercials.

With the perch spawning, my attentions turned once again to bream and just days later I was back, watching the water from the Social swim as darkness fell. I wasn't expecting anything this early in the year, and would have taken a liner as a result, yet come the morning I was on a high as three bream had fallen to the corn stacks over groundbait tactic, the best weighing 12lb 13oz as well as a common of 21lb 15oz. It was a fantastic start that could only get better.

The following week I was back, and being so early in the year the lake was relatively quiet. I managed to drop back into the same swim, which was great as my rods were still marked up from the previous session.

After launching 100 balls of pellet and corn-laced groundbait to a soft spot at the rear of a thin gravel bar at 70 yards, I felt confident that something would happen and sure enough, come darkness the liners started. After landing an 8lb bream at dusk, I found myself playing one of similar size when one of the other indicators started to dance.

Caught while filming for 'Tight Lines'.

At 15lb 3oz, this was the biggest bream of spring 2011.

Knowing that the hooked bream wasn't a monster, I quickly netted it before picking up the other rod and straight away knew that the bream I was attached to was something special. The scales recorded a weight of 15lb 3oz; things were looking good. The night passed without any further action, as did dawn and just after seven I decided to pack up.

Everything had been packed away apart from the rods that lay on the ground, and as I turned to them I noticed that the line had fallen slack on one of them. Picking the rod up, I felt the thump of a good bream and gingerly played it to the net. Halfway in, a clutch on another rod

clicked and I thought this was my line passing over it, yet as I slid the net under a definite double, I noticed that this rod was still knocking. Another bream was on, and after a few minutes I was looking down at two doubles which weighed 10lb 8oz and 12lb 6oz, proof that the last things to pack away should be your rods!

Unfortunately, the Social swim became popular with the carp anglers and I was forced to move around; not that this was a problem as I was able to familiarise myself with new swims. These were usually situated either off the ends of the two main points, or east of these, as this is where the wind blew predominantly.

May proved to be extremely productive and my best catch consisted of 11 double-figure bream, plus numerous carp taken over a two-night stay. However, I was somewhat disappointed that none surpassed the 15lb 4oz fish taken the spring before. My biggest carp was also slightly smaller than the previous season, weighing 28lb 5oz, and knowing that the venue contained plenty of 30s, again I felt somewhat cheated after taking so many. Once June arrived, the bream started to show signs of spawning and I felt it was time to leave the venue alone, once again heading to pastures new.

The extremely dry winters of 2011/12 took their toll on the venue and as a result the river Lavant failed to flow, leaving Westhampnett at least six feet down. When I returned in search of its perch, the gravel bar splitting the lake in two was exposed and although I did catch the odd perch, they failed to show in any numbers. I had intended not to fish the venue during the spring, due to the low water level, but when news came through that CEMEX Angling was looking to sell its portfolio of venues, including Westhampnett, I knew my time on this venue was running out. As they say, one door closes, another opens.

These three doubles came at the same time!

The journey continues

Anyone who has ever written a book will know just how much time it takes. Luckily, the records that I have kept for over a decade have served, not only their intended purpose of quick referencing, but to save hours of what could have been a brain-taxing memory search for dates and figures.

Fortunately, I am methodical and organised, and have managed to keep my sanity by allowing myself to continue my passion between the hours of keyboard- tapping. However, the time consuming campaigns in search of specimen fish have had to be binned and although the venues I try to fish hold the chance of a fish of a lifetime, my mindset has allowed me to enjoy these visits without previously set targets having to be achieved.

The weather has also been on my side. It's been so bad, that sitting at home and watching as the rain consistently falls has reduced the burden of limiting the hours spent bankside. Communicating with other anglers, especially tench anglers, has reinforced the fact that this year has been one of the hardest and most inconsistent on record, so I feel that I haven't missed out too much, and have been fortunate to have picked probably the best possible time to write a book. Other commitments such as guiding, feature producing and giving time to my former sponsors Korum, has, has also taken up valuable angling time and what with having a 'no fishing on the weekend' policy, well, you can start to understand just where my time goes.

Catching dace on the float and pin - proper fishing.

I used to be called the 'quick session specialist' by my previous sponsors. Well, it certainly lives up to its name now. Looking back, it's been an eventful few months. At the start of the year I managed a few trips to my local river Wey in Farnham, and the dace and chub fishing was as good as ever, but picking your moment when you know the river will be carrying some colour is vital. Being able to drop everything, grab the tackle and go is important on such a small river, and on a couple of occasions I even surprised myself by taking upwards of 35lb of dace and chub in just a few hours.

I was also invited to fish the pike Mecca, Chew Valley on a two-day, all expenses paid session with a friend of mine who had been lucky enough to be granted some tickets on his first year of asking. Unfortunately, though the week we fished was one of the worst in Chew's history. I worked it out that for every pike caught during our visit, 220 rod hours were put in, and so to blank after spending 24 fishing hours on its magical banks did soften the disappointment.

Chew, a magical place, but not for me.

I did have one squeaky-bum moment on the first day while fishing from a boat. I had loaded up my reels with 30lb braid and had a rod lying across the boat in each direction. The water was quite rough and suddenly, one of the floats disappeared and the baitrunner burst into life. On striking I was instantly flat-rodded and screaming at my friend to get the net ready. Every now and again the rod would hoop over and the clutch would scream, this was the Chew pike of all time. My friend had managed to get his rods in and the net set up, yet I couldn't make any impression on this fish and with more braid being taken on a tight clutch we decided to up anchor and follow the beast.

After a few anxious minutes, we found ourselves above what we thought was a fish, but it was a snag on the lake bed. Unbeknown to us, the anchor was slipping and every time it did, my rod would hoop over and braid would be taken. We were both completely fooled, and I was redder in the face than my friend, yet this experience did teach me something and that was that I could still get excited from pike fishing, and that's something I didn't think I would ever experience again.

As spring arrived, I headed back down to Westhampnett but although the rains were falling, the River Lavant failed to flow. With the venue six feet or more down, I was reluctant to fish it, yet knowing this might be my last spring on the water decided it couldn't be ignored. There was another factor which I thought would work in my favour. The water level was so low that it might just be easier to locate the bream shoals, but I

Westhampnett in a sorry state.

Westhampnett, one heck of a bream water.

couldn't have been further from the truth, as they seemed to be acting very strangely.

One session I remember well was while set up off the main peninsular, looking toward the boat house. There was an easterly wind blowing, not perfect for bream, but having this blowing straight into my face was perfect. As darkness descended, I watched the water and was amazed to see them rolling in the far eastern corner, which is very uncharacteristic of bream. To make matters worse, if they did decide to move, which I expected them to do in the night, they had to negotiate a ten-kilo pile of Mr Chilcott's boilies! My confidence wasn't high. I did see a few come to the net that night, though, the best a shade over 12lb, yet it

should have been far more. The bream continued to be unpredictable and although I managed a female bream of 14lb 2oz and a male of 13lb 9oz, I never experienced the big hits of previous springs.

It wasn't just the bream that were acting differently. The carp were also noticeable by their absence and where I was catching up to seven a night in the past, over eight overnight sessions I landed just three, two of which were small commons. With things not really happening, the bream going into spawning mode and the unsightly banks around the venue, I decided to call it a day earlier than usual, and as I made my way home I was shocked to see that finally, the River Lavant had started to flow, and it was now the end of May.

Will tonight be the night?

Knowing that CEMEX Angling was selling its venues, I didn't hold out too much hope for a Gold Card dropping through my letter box and a return the following spring, yet amazingly, one did! Thank you, Sue, and at least I know the venue will have some water in it this time.

A forthcoming two-week holiday to the Dominican Republic in June had me frantically trying to finish the main bulk of chapters for this book and it was then that I realised just how little I had completed. Fishing was forgotten about and apart from a few features that had to be done, I locked myself away in my office and burned the midnight oil. Amazingly, on the day before leaving I managed to send over 29 chapters for final proof reading, and to say I needed a holiday... well, I did!

I was totally relaxed on my return and I was hoping that the rudd at Frensham would be obliging, yet apart from one two-pounder that came on a opportunist rod, cast out while guiding a customer, the venue proved to be tough. Well, 'tough' means it wasn't impossible, yet after a number of blank evenings fishing the waggler and sprayed maggot, a better way to describe Frensham would be 'impossible'.

The general feeling was that every venue in the country seemed to be fishing under par, it wasn't just Westhampnett and Frensham that were proving difficult, and it wasn't just stillwaters; most rivers seemed to be suffering as well. For the first time while writing this book, I felt that I wasn't missing out. The rain continued and the catch reports from my contacts failed to raise an eyebrow; this was a good year to be having a break, as such.

These huge F1s came while bream fishing at Willow.

Even my guiding business was suffering, with numerous days having to be rescheduled, and although enquiries were good, many an angler wanted to see an upturn in the weather conditions before booking a date, yet through all this I was never short of things to get on with it.

Knowing that I had limited time, I did make a note of a few things that I wanted to do. One was to investigate the eel potential of Sumners Pond, a day-ticket water on the outskirts of Horsham. Last year, I had taken a customer whose target was to catch an eel, 50% of the national record, and although this wasn't achieved, he did manage two eels over 4lb, a feat in its own right. I was desperate to return and although the venue hasn't

lived up to expectations, I have caught eels to 5lb 5oz, so I shouldn't be disappointed.

Another venture on my list was to gain a basic knowledge of the river Wye. This was more to ease the strain on my time next year on my guiding company, because it seems that everyone wants to catch barbel, yet catching to order down south on rivers such as the Kennet and Loddon is far from easy. It's amazing how much you can learn about a river by just walking the banks and talking to anglers. I have only spent four very long days on this magical river this year, plus a few in the past, yet I feel I already know it quite intimately.

My love for eels will never die.

Dawn on the River Wye.

Time casting a line during these exploratory sessions has been limited, but one morning I caught eight barbel in less than four hours. Now, when, if ever, have I achieved this down south? To be honest, spending two days at a time, sleeping rough, walking, talking and fishing is like going back in time. Once again, I feel like a child on a new adventure, yet now I have the experience to look at a water and understand it. I have two weeks booked with customers on this fantastic river later in the year, which should be a learning curve and set me up for next year.

Has my time on certain stretches of the Loddon come to an end? I think so, as this river is one in serious decline.

If controlling clubs don't wake up and realise that each year the numbers of chub and barbel are falling dramatically, then in five years time they will be almost barren. A policy of introducing just a couple of dozen barbel in the 1lb-plus bracket each year will see year classes filled.

Many won't survive, that's life, but if just a couple go on to adulthood then the angler has something to fish for. The Kennet and Thames are the same; bigger fish but fewer, which is good for the specimen angler, yet the big fish bubble is bursting, and as stretches lose these big fish, few are replacing them.

So as you can see, things are changing. I'm either going to have to look for new stretches that contain more barbel on my local rivers, or start putting in the miles and heading off for longer sessions lasting at least two days elsewhere. This is something that I have tried to do when travelling has been involved over the last couple of years, yet time hasn't allowed this and I end up struggling to find the time for an overnight session, let alone two. Obviously, I have the balance wrong, and even if didn't have the book writing this year, the balance would still be wrong, but luckily, I know this, so at least I can change it.

A Wye barbel taken from the Salmon Hole.

CHAPTER THIRTY-ONE

Guiding: A new direction

It would be wrong not to mention my new direction in angling. When I won the CEMEX Angling Challenge, I promised to put some of my winnings back into angling and this helped to set up my own website www.duncancharman.co.uk. It also allowed me to take a breather, to take a step back and see if it was possible to make a living out of what I love doing.

Image 1: Lewis concentrates for a two-pound roach.

If I were a money man then the answer would have been no, and yet my outlook in life is that if I can cover the bills and spend more time next to water, then this would be good enough for me and for the last two years I have done just that. I may be classified as a full-time angler, but to me that means having the luxury of being on the bank, fishing for myself, 24/7, and my angling is so far from that. Having over 40 years' experience, I felt that it was time to help others, so I set up a guiding service and since doing so, I haven't looked back. Let's take a look at some of the most memorable catches during this time.

Probably the most rewarding aspect has to be working with youngsters, especially those who aren't over-interested in the size of fish they catch, or those just interested in carp, but in how to read a water. They seem to be few and far between these days, so when one shows such a desire, I try to go out of my way to teach them in the same way that my father taught me.

Image 1 shows young Lewis. I met Lewis on the banks of the river Severn at Arley while attending a TCF winner's day. Sitting with his grandfather, I was amazed at this youngster's patience and concentration and, when the tip whacked round, how expertly he placed himself in control of a hard fighting barbel.

Lewis showed a desire to catch a big roach so the following year we got together and headed to River

Farm Fishery in Titchfield. It was one of those tough days, but Lewis stayed focused and for all his efforts should have been rewarded with a big roach, yet it was his grandfather, Barry, who stole the show, landing his dream fish, a 2lb roach. Although it would have been great for Lewis to have landed it, I could see how happy Barry was and young Lewis understood how his grandfather had fished all his life for such a fish and knew that he had plenty of time to do the same.

Image 2 is of James Daxer. James and his brother, Thomas, have been taught the rudiments of angling by their grandfather Mick in very much the same way as I was brought up. No bite alarms and bivvies with these lads, just simple tactics and techniques along with using their senses. James is more at home on still waters but showed an interest in running water and after spending the day with me on the river Loddon, using the pellet lead, he was rewarded with this big chub.

Image 2: Watch the rod tip at all times, James!

Image 3 shows Zac, who requested a night under the stars with me. Heading to Lodge Pond, a runs water that normally produces plenty of singles, he fished the pellet lead to take this 20lb ghostie common. Unfortunately, it didn't go down too well with his father because Kevin has fished the lake on numerous occasions over the past few years and has never caught a carp anywhere close to this one.

Image 3: Zac, in need of a helping hand.

Image 4: Thomas, on sentimental ground.

Image 5: Jake, one to watch in the future.

Image 4 is of Thomas Daxer. The reason I love this photo is that I spent the day with him at Hartley Mauditt, the same farm pond that I grew up fishing and where I learned my skills. Thomas started the day on the pole, catching lots of small carp but every now and again he got smashed up due to fish ploughing through the lily beds. Changing to surface baits on a running line and increasing his line strength soon saw Thomas get the upper hand.

Image 5 shows Jake Curry, one of the most enthusiastic and focused youngsters I have ever met and he has a knack of catching, and not just small fish. His personal best list is impressive, with zander to over 13lb, chub over 6lb, plus big roach, crucians as well as this double-figure barbel that he landed on his first trip for the species. It's not just coarse fishing that Jake likes; he is also an accomplished fly and sea angler - a proper all-rounder and definitely one to watch.

Image 6 is of another keen all-rounder. Oliver Thorn's angling mind never stops; he's thinking all the time. We first met at Old Bury Hill and since that day we

Image 6: Ollie with a zander from Old Bury Hill.

have fished successfully for zander, chub and crucian carp, yet it's a big perch that Olli desires most and, come the winter, I know exactly the place to go.

Image 7 shows young Jack Shorter. Living very close to me, I found Jack on my doorstep requesting a day's fishing. Knowing I might just be able to keep his concentration for around two hours, I needed a venue that would give some instant action and with Gold Valley on our doorstep, we headed there. I think it took just five minutes for Jack to get almost pulled in by this mirror. He now has his own rod and reel, he's that keen.

Image 7: The smile says it all.

Image 8: Don't tell Dad what you've just caught.

Image 9: Cold, but well worth the effort.

Image 8 is my godson, Max. We spent the day roving the river Loddon with Chris Ponsford, and after setting him up in a swim that I call the 'five-pound chub swim' he was soon bent into this beauty that weighed 5lb 9oz. Once again, it didn't go down too well with Dad whose best is 5lb 4oz!

Image 9 proves that sometimes you have to go to extreme measures to catch a personal best. Nick booked me after seeing my results catching rudd in the winter. Braving the cold, and I recall it was cold, we headed to Frensham one February afternoon. Fishing into evening using helicopter rigs and wading out into the cold water, Nick was rewarded with a few rudd, although his best dropped just short of our target, a two-pounder.

Image 10 shows one of my regulars, Mel. Although I didn't take this picture or was even present at the time, I know that Mel would agree that I did have some influence in its caplure, as the week before we had used the same tactics, on the same

Image 10: Words of wisdom.

venue, during one of the hottest days of the year. Failing to catch, I told Mel to return when the weather changed, which he did the following week and, using the same approach, he banked two big grass carp.

Image 11 features Dave, who had never caught a barbel before. After booking me, we headed to the Loddon and after missing a number of chub bites, the tip flew round and he found himself attached to this double. Unfortunately, the fish snagged him and with only one option, I had to strip of to my pants and jump in. It was late in the year and not only was the water cold but also the swim was far deeper than I had envisaged, yet there was no way I was going to let this one win.

Image 11: The naked guide!

Image 12: Natural talent.

Image 12 shows another angler with a natural knack of landing big fish. Martin is a regular and we team up on numerous occasions each year with the view to landing specimens of a variety of species.

Martin's personal best is impressive and although he may say that his best fish caught with me is a 6lb 10oz chub, I think that it should be this big perch. It came after a slow start in a normally productive swim. Martin asked what I would do in such a situation and I said 'move', which we did, and we caught. Martin is a very good listener and has patience - a very good combination if you want to catch consistently.

Image 13 shows Mark, who is better known for catching the lake record zander from Old Bury Hill weighing 16lb 2oz. However, it's not just this fish that stands out, as we spent the night roach fishing at River Farm Fishery. Luckily, we timed our arrival perfectly as days later the roach started to spawn, yet during our trip we lost count of the amount of big roach we caught, which included this brace of twos.

Well, there you have it, a few examples of why anglers book a guide, over 40 years of experience revealed in a day. It's not always plain sailing with rods bent and clutches screaming. There are days when it's impossible, something in the air switches the fish off the feed and whatever we try fails to trigger a response, yet on these rare occasions I do offer a return visit. It's a policy I don't like offering, hence why I try my hardest to ensure that the angler catches fish during the day, and one that I haven't had to use often. Even on a hard day, I seem to manage to get a fish or two interested.

The enjoyment I get out of helping others to catch is beyond words, yet although I feel I'm a competent guide, when a customer hooks a big fish, I'm like a bad passenger in a car; I feel out of control and on occasions have been told to calm down. I don't think there is a coarse species in this country I can't cater for, and I've even guided anglers when eel fishing; certainly not an easy task. The barbel weeks on the Wye are going to be a real eye-opener, and a species I will be looking out for when I am there is pike, as this is the river to fish if you want a 30.

Image 13: A dream comes true.

Watching an angler land a personal best and then seeing the joy as they lift it in front of a lens is addictive, but even more enjoyable is when anglers send me photos of fish they've caught on their own, after spending the day with me.

If you're struggling for results, getting back into the sport after a break or need to find out all there is to know about a stretch, then hiring a guide is a viable solution.

For more details check out my website
www.duncancharman.co.uk

Doing what I do best!